A MANUAL OF DEMONOLOGY AND THE OCCULT

Kent A. Philpott, MDiv, DMin

EVP

Earthen Vessel Publishing

MANUAL OF DEMONOLOGY AND THE OCCULT

©2021 by Kent Philpott
First published 1973, Library of Congress Catalog Card Number:
73-8363

All rights reserved.
Earthen Vessel Media, LLC
San Rafael, CA 94903
www.earthenvesselmedia.com

ISBN: 978-1-946794-26-0 print
        978-1-946794-27-7 eBook

Library of Congress Control Number: 2021935754
Transcribed by Margaret Bates
Cover design by Mary Keydash
Interior design by KLC Philpott

All Biblical Scripture quotations, unless otherwise indicated, are taken from the Holy Bible, English Standard Version® (ESV®), copyright © 2001 by Crossway Bibles, a publishing ministry of Good News Publishers. All rights reserved.

Contents

Prefaces

PREFACE TO THE ORIGINAL

In March of 1967 I began a street ministry in San Francisco's Haight-Ashbury District. It was the beginning of the hippie culture, the start of the drug scene; and it was there that I began encountering Satan. One of my first experiences was an example of satanic mind control. A man about 50 years of age, bizarrely dressed with a wild tangle of hair on his head and face, was standing on Haight Street directly across the street. His eyes were wide open, but he appeared to be in some sort of trance. I stood in front of him and looked straight into his eyes, yet he gave no indication that he was aware of me. Following his gaze, I found he was staring at a very pretty girl on the opposite sidewalk. Crossing the street, I stood alongside the girl and tried to figure out what was going on. The girl was wearing only a loose-fitting sheet. She had been painted—her whole body—with a wild array and arrangement of colors. And she was in a deep trance from which I could not budge her. A strong sense of evil pervaded the scene; I became convinced that the old man held some strange power over her. I left, bewildered but determined to find out what I could about the trances. It led me into a study of the occult.

Ever since those early days in the Haight-Ashbury, my ministry has been largely to the hip culture, and occultism has continually shown itself to be a major facet of that movement. I have witnessed dozens of satanic incidents and cases of demon possession. Having learned to think like a modern man, I had trouble analyzing the similarities and dissimilarities between contemporary demonology and biblical demonology. At first, occult expressions I observed seemed no more than crude, anachronisms in a scientific, technological society.

My problem was how to approach the matter. Through the years the Bible has proven to me to be useful in understanding and dealing with demonology.

By demonology I mean the study of the demonic, the study of the satanic. Under the heading of demonology I include such occult practices as astrology, magic, fortune-telling, spiritualism, necromancy, Satanism, clairvoyance, telepathy, astral projection, psychokinesis, and similarities to and variations of these basic patterns. Extrasensory perception operates through the agency of Satan, while hypnosis may or may not be used in such a way as to classify it with the occult.

While I believe that the occult is demonic, the connection between the two is not automatic. I am convinced that the occult works through satanic power. The account of the girl with a "spirit of divination," in Acts 16, provides a connection between the occult and the demonic since divination is fortune-telling (an occult practice), and Paul cast the evil spirit out of the girl.

I accept the biblical passages dealing with the demonic as authentic and directly applicable to and understanding of contemporary occult and demonic practices. Several options are always open to the interpreter of biblical materials, and I have chosen one such option. It is simply a direct approach to the material without any attempt to demythologize, existentialize, or psychologize the account.

In line, then, with the biblical material, I am assuming the reality of Satan and demons. The reality of demons may someday be demonstrable scientifically, but I am not trying to prove their existence.

It is not my concern to present a theology of demonology. The intent is to deal with the data—the demonic activities, both biblical and extrabiblical. I am not concerned about the "how" or the "why" of Satan and the demonic. That Satan and the demons already are is my assumption, and I am working from there.

Kent Philpott
1972

PREFACE TO THE CURRENT EDITION

It has come time to update and expand our written offerings and our work in this important arena of deliverance ministry. The reader will note in the Preface to the original edition of this book published by Zondervan Publishing House in 1973 that I said my ministry regarding demonization and deliverance was largely to the "hip" culture. In the decades since then, American culture in general has been overrun with "contemporary occultism," a term that is now in the common lexicon.

Along with the re-publication of this book, which was originally a Masters thesis, we also call attention to two other books we are presenting on this topic: *Deliver Us from Evil: How Jesus Casts Out Demons Today* (Earthen Vessel Publishing, 2014) and *A Deliverance Handbook* (Earthen Vessel Publishing, 2021). These books are meant to equip others to engage in deliverance ministry, because we are unable to directly and in person minister to all who seek relief from demonic influence.

We also have produced audio/visual material to accompany the books or to use separately, available via VOD (Video On Demand) in various venues and via audio on most popular podcast platforms. A list of where to find these presentations can be found at earthenvesselmedia.com. It is our hope that many Christians and others caught in Satan's web of deception will gain new insight and develop new discernment about what the devil's goal has always been—to separate mankind from faith in God and His Son, Jesus.

It is also our hope that many who would otherwise feel pressured to enlist the paid help of a professional claiming ability to dispel or exorcise oppressive demons will instead seek help from those who perform this service as a free ministry.

Feel free to contact us at info@earthenvesselmedia.com

Kent Philpott
2021

Hitler is not a single personality but two that inhabit the same body. The one is very soft and sentimental and indecisive. The other is hard, cruel and decisive. The first weeps at the death of a canary; the second cries that "there will be no peace in the land until a body hangs from every lamppost…nothing but death, annihilation and hatred."

WALTER LANGER
The Mind of Adolf Hitler

1
Introduction: The Problem

There is something fascinating about the occult. Man's earliest history reveals his involvement in strange practices of witchcraft and demon worship. Down through the ages, in most every nation, the occult has grasped a foothold. No culture has "progressed" to the point of leaving it behind. America has seen an explosion of the demonic unparalleled in recent history. It may be seen in the titles of many movies. *The Devils, Spirits of the Dead, Beast of the Yellow Night, Necromancy, The Cry of the Banshee, Creature with the Blue Hand*, and *Werewolves on Wheels* have been shown recently in motion picture theaters across the nation.

Occult Influence

Indeed a revival of the demonic is steeping the land. Susy Smith, in her book, *Today's Witches*, says, "The truth is that witchcraft is having its greatest resurgence since the Middle Ages."[1] The statistics of the movement are impressive. *The San Francisco Chronicle* reports that six million Americans are devoted followers of the occult and twenty-five million patronize astrologers. An article by Donald Nugent in a recent church publication provides further indications of the size of the occult involvement: "Though statistics are probably not very reliable, there are an estimated 60,000 sorcerers in France, 30,000 witches in England and within the five years, 20,000 Satanists in the United States." Nugent's figures are not so recent as Smith's and are probably well below the actual involvement. The American culture has been

---

[1] Susy Smith, *Today's Witches* (Englewood Cliffs, N. J." Prentice Hall, Inc., 1971), p. 1.

so saturated with the occult in recent months that the mass media interest in the occult continues to grow. Occult involvement in the San Francisco Bay Area cuts across several strata of population. Young, old and middle-aged people are involved. High school students, many from stable and wealthy homes, are actively practicing satanic arts. The occult has a broad base and can be expected to spread to small and large communities all across America. We are observing something unusual—the acceptance of the occult on a broad cultural base. Previously the occult was an underground movement.

The vast amount of literature on the demonic is evident to most Americans. There are books on satanic subjects in many supermarkets; occult bookshops are opening across the country. Television has become a medium for the occult with programs such as the weekly ABC network series called "The Sixth Sense." Many of NBC's "Night Gallery" shorts, hosted by Rod Serling, have an occult theme; the same network's "Ghost Story" that began in the fall of 1972 also deals in some measure with this subject. Two of ABC's long-running offerings, "Bewitched" and "Dark Shadows," have a pronounced occult theme. Courses in witchcraft are a part of many college curricula. And one crystal ball gazer in Washington, D. C., advises some of our top political leaders. The occult has become a multi-million-dollar business.

Young people are particularly caught up in this mania. Interest in magic, fortune-telling, and astrology followed close on the heels of drugs and Eastern religions in the Haight-Ashbury's hippie subculture of 1967 through 1970.[2] Theodore Roszak states the occult "has become an integral part of the counter culture." But drugs and Oriental religions do not always share the same stage with the demonic. It is middle class America and the over-thirty age group that participate most avidly in occultism's revival. The current interest in the occult goes far beyond the youth culture and extends into many phases of American life.

FOUR APPROACHES IN UNDERSTANDING THE DEMONIC

The interest in the occult raises questions concerning the reality of

---

[2] Theodore Roszak, *The Making of a Counter Culture* (Garden City, N. Y.: Doubleday & Co., Anchor Books, 1969), pp. 124-25.

the demonic. Everyone confronted by it must come to terms with it in some manner. Certainly a number of options of understanding are open. The Christian sees the occult as a problem especially because of the place given the demonic in the Bible. For the contemporary Christian, the subject of the occult or demonology presents a problem in need of careful examination.

Apart from a Christian understanding of the demonic, there are at least three rival positions. Let it be understood that these positions are not the only possible answers to demonology. They do serve, however, to outline the major approaches.

THE ANIMIST APPROACH.

First of all, it has been argued that contemporary belief in demons is a holdover from primitive animism. Animism is "the belief that all natural phenomena are possessed of souls or spirits that animate them and explain their special characteristics."[3] The history of belief in spirits goes back to the most ancient of peoples. There is no culture that has not had a history of religion and magic; this magic is a device used for protection against "evil" spirits or for gaining help from "good" spirits. Edward Langton, and expert in demonology, says, "Belief in the existence of evil spirits has prevailed among all the known peoples of the world from the earliest of time of which we have any knowledge."[4]

It is thought that animism forms the backdrop of all religion and that contemporary religions have evolved from primitive animistic beliefs. Animism is seen as a crude form of belief based on an erroneous understanding of the physical universe. Those who hold this view believe that superstition, an anachronism among peoples who formally hold to a more advanced religious and scientific world view.

Such a view dismisses the reality of spirits except as they exist in the minds of people. A modified form of this is held by some Christians who disallow the reality of Satan and demons; these do not take demonology too seriously.

A school friend of mine started working with a group of young

---

[3] Van A. Harvey, *A Handbook of Theological Terms* (New York: The Macmillan Co., 1964), p. 22.

[4] Edward Langton, *Essentials of Demonology* (London: The Epworth Press, 1949), p. 219.

people in nearby Oakland. We had had a few friendly arguments about the reality of demons. He thought it was all superstition, a hold-over from primitive animism. But one day, one of the young fellows in his group confessed to conducting séances. He also confessed to having a guide spirit (a demon). He asked for prayer. Some of the others prayed for him right then, and the demon began manifesting itself. The subject screamed, contorted his face, doubled up, and fell to the floor. Prayer for him continued. In a few short minutes the struggle was over. The demon was gone, and my friend had observed the casting out of a demon.

In short, primitive man believed in one God, but this belief gradually became perverted into animism and black magic.

The psychological approach. A second approach to demonology, somewhat like the animistic view, is the psychological approach. This particular view has so many variations that only a simple outline of the essentials can be presented here.

THE PSYCHOLOGICAL VIEW

This view declares there is no concrete basis to biblical demonology. One holding to this view would say that attributing satanic causes to bizarre behavior is simply poor and ancient psychology. It explains away the biblical references to demons as no more than cultural expressions which were appropriate for that age. It views demon possession as some type of neurosis, psychosis, or other emotional illness; Jesus' encounters with demon-possessed people were in reality Jesus encountering and ministering to the mentally ill. Kurt Koch, a Christian minister who is widely experienced with the occult, illustrates the psychological approach by saying, "Possessed persons are compulsive neurotics, who are ruled by an intensive psychic process without themselves accepting this process."[5]

The work of the parapsychologist is relevant at this point. There seems to be two schools of thought among the parapsychologists. Some think they are observing and measuring actual spiritual phenomena, while others maintain they are observing and measuring

---

[5] Kurt Koch, *Christian Counseling and Occultism* (Grand Rapids: Kregel Publications, 1965), p. 184.

normal psychical (non-spiritual) phenomenon that at present cannot be fully explained.

The psychological approach to demonology dismisses the reality of any external spiritual demonic influence or power.

THE DUALISTIC APPROACH.

A third approach to demonology can be designated by the title "dualism." Ancient Zoroastrianism was dualistic in that it pictured two gods who were equal, each counterbalancing the other. One was a "good" god while the other was "bad." Christian theology has at time been described as dualistic because of the doctrine of God and Satan. But knowledgeable Christians are not comfortable with any sort of dualism, since the Bible does not teach it. Scripture presents Satan as a created, defeated rebel who is against the only true and living God.

The occultist may find a comfortable philosophical frame-work in dualism. Both the good and the bad gods may have at their disposal numerous angels, spirits, or demons, and both may seek worship in dualistic thinking. None of the spirits are seen as necessarily evil; the bad spirits simply need careful handling by means of magic. Both gods are equal in power and authority, each demanding religious observance or devotions. In dualism a spirit, good or bad, is still an authentic spirit. The bad are to be avoided or appeased, the good are to be sought or worshiped. But both actions usher the practitioner directly into the occult.

One day I picked up a young hitchhiker on the freeway. I was listening to the radio, and he asked me to turn up the volume.

"Boy, that song is good," he said. "They really have power—it's the power of Satan. Do you believe in Satan?

"Yes," I replied, then I continued, "Do you believe in God?"

"Oh, yes. But I worship Satan, because he's in control of things now."

This type of modern dualism must be dealt with. Christians need solid answers to such flimsy philosophy.

THE BIBLICAL APPROACH

The Bible provides an alternative to the tree previous approaches to demonology. Satan is presented in the Bible as a real entity, having certain personal attributes. The Bible writer never takes Satan for granted; he is taken seriously. Satan is seen as an enemy of God who is able to influence men and their environment within limits. Satan is not omnipresent but works through demons. While demons in the New Testament are neither impotent nor irrational, they are always evil and are ruled by the devil. Joseph Bayly writes, "Demons are invisible, but real, spiritual beings who are under the control of Satan, 'prince of the devils.'"[6]

The presence of Jesus often frightened and excited demons. In the Bible demons are even found responding verbally to Him. They could be cast out of the possessed and ordered not to speak.

> So they came to the other side of Lake Galilee, to the territory of the Gerasenes. As soon as Jesus got out of the boat he was met by a man who came out of the burial caves. This man had an evil spirit in him and lived among the graves. Nobody could keep him tied with chains any more; many times his feet and hands had been tied, but every time he broke the chains, and smashed the irons on his feet. He was two strong for anyone to stop him! Day and night he wandered among the graves and through the hills, screaming and cutting himself with stones.
>
> He was some distance away when he saw Jesus; so he ran, fell on his knees before him, and screamed in a loud voice, "Jesus, Son of the Most High God! What do you want with me? For God's sake, I beg you, don't punish me!" (He said this because Jesus was saying to him, "Evil spirit, come out of this man!") So Jesus asked him, "What is your name?" The man answered, "My name is 'Mob'—there are so many of us!" And he kept begging Jesus not to send the evil spirits out of the territory.
>
> A large herd of pigs was near by, feeding on the hillside. The spirits begged Jesus, "Send us to the pigs, and let us go into them." So he let them. The evil spirits went out of the man and went into the pigs. The whole herd—about two thousand pigs in all—rushed down the side of the cliff into the lake and were drowned.

[6] Joseph Bayly, *What About Horoscopes?* (Elgin, Ill. David C. Cook Publishing Co., 1970), p. 41

The men who had been taking care of the pigs ran away and spread the news in the town and among the farms. The people went out to see what had happened. [7]

Thus, a biblical approach to demonology accepts the reality of demons and Satan.

PRECAUTIONARY NOTE

Among Christians it seems there have been two ways of dealing with the subject of the demonic that lacks a biblical perspective. One is the exaggeration of the role of the demonic and man's susceptibility to the influence of Satan. A biblical understanding avoids attributing all problems—physical, emotional, or circumstantial—to the direct agency of demons. Jesus' words and ministry distinguished physical problems from demon activity. The claim, "The devil made me do it," can easily excuse one from facing personal responsibilities.

A second approach that lacks a biblical perspective is to minimize the role of Satan, sometimes to the point of dismissing him altogether. This is done only by sacrificing a balanced biblical attitude. Satan and his demons are not dismissed in the Bible, and demonic activity is seen as a reality needing to be dealt with.

Many Christians at this time are struggling for a better understanding of Satan. They need help in understanding and ministering to the thousands all about us who are caught up in today's massive revival of the occult.

DISCUSSION QUESTIONS

1. How is the current rise in demonism different from previous outbreaks of demonism?

2. What are some causes of the current rise in demonism today?

3. What are some possible connections between the occult and Eastern religions?

4. Animism is a major world religion. Animistic people tend to be superstitious and easily influenced by the occult. How does

---

[7] Mark 5:1–14 *Good News for Modern Man*

animism affect occult belief and practice? How does the animistic approach to demonology conflict with the biblical approach?

5. Probably the major modern non-Christian approach to demonology is the psychological approach. Can a Christian psychologist accept the reality of the demonic? Explain.

6. Describe a modern dualist. How might a dualist react to a biblical approach to demonology?

7. How does the biblical approach to demonology answer the important questions arising from the current resurgence of the occult?

8. Can the Christian have an unhealthy interest in demonology? How can a Christian achieve a healthy view of the demonic?

I like killing people because it is more fun than killing wild game in the forest, because man is the most dangerous animal of all. To kill something gives me the most thrilling experience...the best part of it is that when I die, I will be reborn in paradise, and all that I have killed will become my slaves. I will not give you my name because you will try to slow me down or stop my collecting of slaves for my after-life.

THE ZODIAC

2
Theological Problems of Demonology

Several theological problems come into focus when the subject of demonology is discussed concerning the nature of the demonic and the place given to it in the Bible. These problem areas can be approached only in a most simple manner here, but their discussion is important to a reasonable examination of demonology.

THE PROBLEM OF INTERPRETATION

The outcome of any biblical study depends upon the method of interpretation applied to the material. This is especially true in the case of demonology. In the Church historically, more than one method has been employed for interpreting the Scriptures related to this subject. Each method was intended to provide a useful tool for dealing with the matter.

DEMYTHOLOGIZING

The first method of interpretation under discussion is demythologizing. To say that one demythologizes the demonic accounts means a denial of any external or objective reality for either Satan or demons.[1] The concept of Satan and evil spirits is seen by a proponent of this

---

[1] Demythologizing means to take the "mythical" (usually supernatural) elements out of a Scripture passage and interpret the passage apart from the "myth." A demythologizer would say the truth of the Bible is expressed in outmoded forms, so that the Bible needs to be reinterpreted using more scientific, modern understanding. Concerning the Resurrection, the demythologizer would say the myth element is the bodily resurrection of Jesus; the true resurrection is the message of Jesus "rising" in the hearts of the disciples.

view as an attempt by ancient men to personalize or externalize their experience of evil, fear, bizarre events, or tragic circumstances.

For the demythologizer, Jesus' temptation, recorded in Matthew 4, was not an actual, objective encounter with a being named Satan, but was actually Jesus' subjective encounter with evil. The myth about the temptation of Jesus is seen as the aspect of Satan in personal contact with Jesus. Removing the myth element, though not denying the struggle Jesus went through, reveals for the demythologizer the core of the story—Jesus' struggle against evil. The personification of evil in the form of Satan is seen as a myth.

The demythologizer has come to his position in an attempt to solve theological problems. Rudolf Bultmann expressed the idea that most of the mythology relating to the demonic was derived from Gnosticism. But the central point is that Satan's reality along with the reality of any demons is dismissed. There is no "Satan" to deal with. Satan becomes only a mythical character, one who has no objective (physical or spiritual) reality.

EXISTENTIALIZING

A second way of interpreting the demonic material in the Bible is to existentialize it. This does not necessarily mean that an external reality for Satan and demons is denied. On the other hand, the demonic is not usually dealt with as an external reality by an interpreter using the existential method. Whether the demonic is real is not the important thing to him; that evil exists and that men do encounter it, however, is important. The existentialist can be a demythologizer, but the thrust of existentialism lies in the meaning of the demonic to a person encountering it.

Paul Tillich serves as an example of a theologian who existentialized the demonic. Tillich denied the reality of Satan and demons and saw man's attempt to be a "god" as the core of the demonic. It is man's encountering his finiteness and relating to it as final that caused Tillich to refer to the demonic. If man had never acted in such a way the demonic would have no reality at all but would only be existentially possible.

Evidence for the reality of the demonic can be seen in every aspect of the life of man, according to the existentialist. He may or may not deny any kind of personal or objective reality for the demonic, yet he

takes the demonic seriously. While not denying their reality, and existentialist would probably not engage in casting out demons.

POPULAR WORLD VIEWS

Another way to interpret demonology is to adopt any one of a number of world views that are generally non-theological in nature. For
instance, asserting that all talk of demons is simply resorting to pagan
superstitions, or that it is nonscientific, is to adopt a modern, popular
world view.

One may say that Jesus simply accommodated Himself to the idea
of demons held by people of His day, but that He Himself knew better. Edward Langton offers an important word in regard to this view
that Jesus merely accepted His contemporaries' erroneous view of
demons:

> He knew that no such creatures existed. It cannot be doubt-
> ed that the disciples of Jesus, and those who have reported
> and preserved His teaching, were firmly convinced that their
> own beliefs upon this subject were shared in all sincerity by
> Jesus. Not only did Jesus fail to correct or deny those beliefs;
> throughout His ministry, by word and deed, He also empha-
> sized them, and solemnly conferred upon His disciples the
> power to cast out evil spirits.[2]

Or one may say that Jesus did not know any better Himself, but
that we know better. We know demons do not exist.

Or again, one may say demonology does not belong to theology at all but really should be considered in the field of psychology.
It has been argued that there is no such thing as demonic influence
over individuals, but rather that individuals said to be suffering from
Satan's influence are really suffering psychologically, and therefore no
external spiritual cause is to be considered.

Another world view is advance by occultists who maintain there
really are spiritual beings that can influence man. Such a view declares
there are three classes of spirits: good, neutral, and evil. (Occasionally
the neutral class is dropped.) These spirits are "communicated" with

---

[2] Edward Langton, *Essentials of Demonology* (London: The Epworth Press,
1949), p. 160.

through such practices as white and black magic, fortune-telling, spiritualism (séances), among others. One holding this view might refer to Jesus as a "great medium" who knew how to control the spirits. This view accepts the concept of demons (Satan's existence may be denied) but would refer to them as spirits. Contact with these spirits (good, neutral, or evil) is neither necessarily discouraged nor considered non-biblical or anti-Christian in nature.

THE BIBLICAL APPROACH

A fourth method of interpreting the demonic is a basic acceptance of the Bible as it stands. In the introduction, I made a brief statement of this method of interpretation. The conclusions I have reached concerning the demonic are based on a simple, literal approach to the biblical material.

THE PROBLEM OF DUALISM

What is the place of Satan and demons in Christian thought? Some have objected that to recognize Satan and demons as real entities is to decide for a dualistic theology. That is, Satan, representing evil, opposes God, who represents good; good versus evil or a good God versus an evil god. This is a complicated problem, since it involves the concept of the sovereignty of God.

A fundamental tenet of biblical Christianity is that God is sovereign, that He is Lord, ruler, and ultimate in authority and power. God is almighty God. And this is a solid biblical picture of God: He is sovereign. But where does the devil fit in? Why does God allow Satan to exercise power and authority in His universe?

First of all, the Bible does not present a theological dualism. God and Satan are not presented as equal forces battling for leadership or power. There is no unhealthy dualism in biblical demonology. Satan is seen as a fallen creature, under the condemnation as well as the authority of God. Satan is a defeated enemy. God alone is Creator, while Satan is not creative but rather destructive and immoral.[3]

Satan does have a power to which men are potentially vulnerable. Man can even be possessed (demonized) by Satan or demons. Satan

---

[3] The following biblical passages describe Satan's position: Matthew 25:41; Luke 9:1; 10:17; Hebrews 2:14; 1 John 3:8; 4:4; Revelation 12:11; 20:10.

can accuse the "brethren,"[4] but man can effectively resist him.[5] The Bible pictures God as sovereign and at the same time allows Satan certain limited and conditioned access to man. Merrill Unger writes: "Demonology as portrayed in the Bible is consistent with the doctrine of the sovereignty of God."[6] Satan is never in danger of overthrowing God, but he is opposed to God. The outcome of the opposition is not in question: Satan has already lost and Christ is the victor.

Satan exists and exercises power in the freedom of God. God freely allows Satan to be Satan, but Satan cannot move outside the limits God, in His freedom, has laid down. Man is not unwillingly subject to Satan; he must place himself at the disposal of Satan by yielding to sin. Such submission of man to Satan is allowed by God. God warns us to resist Satan and demon practices, but man is free to disobey.

In the New Testament stories of the demon-possessed, those possessed are not always completely controlled to the point that they cannot seek deliverance.[7] Even the possessed are not permanently under the control of Satan, and the condition can be instantly reversed through the power of God.

The question of why God allows Satan to exist and have power has not been answered, because the Bible does not deal with the question as such. The answer has to do with the freedom God has given His creation, even the freedom to rebel against Him. Satan is simply pictured as existing and having certain limited influence with men.

The great Bible teacher, Lewis Sperry Chafer, sees Satan as a fallen being—an unholy archangel.[8] Using Ezekiel 28:11–19 and Isaiah 14:12–17, he shows Satan's early history, that of a ruling angel who had the freedom to disobey God. He pictures God casting Satan out of heaven as a result of a rebellion. Chafer believes demons are angels who followed Satan in this rebellion against God. These demons likewise had the freedom to withstand God and disobey Him. The

---

[4] Revelation 12:10

[5] James 4:7

[6] Merrill F. Unger, *Biblical Demonology* (Wheaton, Ill." Scripture Press, 1952), p. 25.

[7] In the following passages it can be noted that possessed or demonized people were able to exercise free will: Mark 5:1-13 and Acts 16:16-18.

[8] Lewis Sperry Chafer, *Systematic Theology* (Dallas, Tex.: Dallas Seminary Press, 1947), vol. 2, pp. 34–35.

demons are said to be bodiless spirits or spiritual beings (not flesh and blood). They are beings, objective reality in the spiritual realm, and they are intelligent beings. But they are completely ruled by Satan and are required to carry out the will of Satan. The purpose of Satan and demons is to hinder the will of God. Satan and his host are clever in that they adapt themselves to changing situations and times. Chafer says they are "adapting the manner of their activity to the enlightenment of the age and locality attacked."[9]

In keeping with the New Testament style, Chafer believes demons can possess bodies today as in the first century. They can also make themselves to appear as "angels of light,"[10] just as Satan can.

Chafer rules out any dualism. Satan can only attempt to copy the divine attributes of God, yet he alone is rather powerless to accomplish such a counterfeit without the aid of his demons. And for Chafer, Jesus Christ is clearly victor over the demonic forces, through His death and resurrection.

THE PROBLEM OF DISEASE

Matthew's comment on Jesus' ministry in Syria highlights an important distinction between physical (medical) disease and the demonic. The passaged reads: "So his fame spread throughout all Syria, and they brought him all the sick, those afflicted with various diseases and pains, demoniacs, epileptics, and paralytics, and he healed them."[11] Thus, the Bible draws a difference between those who were medically sick and those who were demonized. When Jesus sent out the twelve disciples, He gave them authority over unclean spirits, and infirmity.[12] In Mark 7 we find Jesus casting a demon out of a little girl,[13] but healing a man who was deaf and had a speech impediment.[14] Jesus ministered differently according to the situation. In Mark 9 Jesus cast a demon out of a person who appeared to display symptoms sometimes

---

[9] Ibid, p. 117.

[10] 2 Corinthians 11:14

[11] Matthew 4:24

[12] Matthew 10:1; see also Luke 9:1.

[13] Mark 7:24–30

[14] Mark 7:31–37

associated with epilepsy.[15] Jesus did not cast demons out of people who were sick—He healed them. He ministered to the demonized by casting the spirits out. Jesus knew the difference between disease and the demonic.[16]

The distinction between the diseased and the demonized is not always so easy to see in the world today. Some Christians attribute every unhealthy state to demons, while, on the other hand, some Christians deny the possibility of the demonic being the cause of any illness or emotional problem or lying behind any sort of bizarre behavior. The picture is further complicated by the fact that the demonized and the mentally ill often share similar behavioral symptoms. Satan characteristically attacks a person's thoughts and feelings, but especially does Satan seek to direct a person's will. It is only when a person's will has been largely (though not necessarily completely) taken over by Satan that he can be said to be truly demonized. But because Satan works on a person's thoughts and feelings it may be impossible to distinguish clearly between physical illness and the demonic.

MENTAL ILLNESS

A researcher into the area of mental illness and the demonic will find that sources and documentation are scarce. The Bible itself does not provide enough solid material on mental illness and the demonic to help formulate any clear distinctions between the two. Although some New Testament cases of demonization do have characteristics similar to modern illness. The Bible is largely silent on the matter. Yet, there is a need to distinguish between emotionally disturbed persons and those influenced by Satan. The following attempt to draw that distinction is based on my personal observations and pastoral work on the word of Alfred Lechler.

Doctor Lechler is a Christian psychiatrist who has had wide clinical experience upon which to base his observations. He collected his data from his own psychiatric counseling practice. Lechler accepts the biblical picture of Satan as it stands. As one who takes demons

---

[15] Mark 9:14–29. Epilepsy is discussed farther on in this section.

[16] Additional references: Mark 1:32–34; 3:10, 6:13; Luke 7:21, 9:1. Acts 8:7 indicates that in the ministry of one of the early Christians, Philip, a distinction was drawn between disease and the demonic.

seriously, he sees a distinction between mental illness and behavior that is essentially demonic.

It is plain that many similarities exist between some forms of mental illness and demonic symptoms. A person suffering from the psychological disorder termed schizophrenia may exhibit bizarre symptoms in that he may feel he is being persecuted, perhaps by demons, or that he has been hypnotized, or even that demons are living inside him. He may be rebellious, and he may be suffering from depression, anxiety, and thoughts of suicide. These symptoms are more typically characteristics of the schizophrenic than the demonized. The talk of demonic influence may lead one to suspect such a person is demonized, but in general, a truly demonized person rarely refers to his possession by demons; in fact, he is usually ignorant of any influence of Satan in his life. A demonized person may be aware that spiritual forces influence him, even indwell him, but he will not consider such spirits to be demonic or evil. Such a person may refer to guide spirits, familiar spirits, good or neutral spirits, but rarely refer to the spirits as demonic.

Lechler provides a very helpful principle at this point. He says, "It is almost invariably true to say that if a person is forever talking about being possessed, he is really suffering from some form of mental illness rather than from a demonic influence.[17]

A young man I encountered had used drugs for some time and appeared to be emotionally disturbed. He spent hours in meditation and paid serious attention to his daily horoscope. He said he could see a pyramid over his head as he meditated. It was said he could speak several dozen languages. He appeared to be emotionally disturbed. However, after he received Christian counseling, the demonic nature of the young man's problem became evident. What appeared to be an emotional problem turned out to be demonic.

Lechler also feels that a psychologically ill person's delusions regarding demons come from "—his having read or heard something concerning demons or the demonic either before or at the onset of his illness."[18]

---

[17] Kurt Koch, *Occult Bondage and Deliverance* (Grand Rapids: Kregel Publications, 1970), p. 155. To this book Doctor Lechler has contributed a major section dealing with the demonic's relation to disease.

[18] Ibid.

An actual case of demonization affects certain results in the victim's life. Generally such a person dislikes Bible reading, prayer, and Christian fellowship, and he will seek to avoid contact with Christians. Also, there may be strong impulses to curse God or Christian symbols and compulsions to disturb Christian meetings. These symptoms generally do not hold for the psychologically ill.

One night a girl came to a small Bible study I was conducting. She had been involved in fortune-telling, and later she said that she had a strange desire to swear, shout, and curse God during the Bible study. Only her fear of embarrassment kept her from it. She was converted that night and told of a long involvement in the occult, through which she had become demon-possessed.

The mentally ill will usually have no trouble in speaking of Jesus, and if people try to cast demons out of such a person, he will not be overly upset by it and no evident change of behavior will result. Mental illness, rather than demonization, may be suspected if there has been no direct involvement in the occult, association with a heretical Christian cult, or long term commitment to obvious sin.

I have often mistaken mental illness for demon possession. Several years ago I encountered two young people who appeared to be demon-possessed. All attempts at casting out the suspected demons proved valueless. Now, after several years of growing as Christians, both young people are living normal, healthy lives. Their problem proved not to be demon possession.

Hallucinations are common to some forms of mental illness and are much more common to mental illness than to demon-possession. The mentally ill person may suffer from hallucinations in which he hears voices, or the patient may engage in speaking to unseen persons. Yet this kind of speaking and hearing usually is marked by unnatural or nonsensical content. A person may begin to think he should stop eating or dressing, or even that he should kill himself. There may be compulsions to engage in religious activities. Delusions such as hearing voices or speaking to strange people are characteristic of mental illness but are also found with the demon-possessed.

Looking over case histories of a recent two-month period I discovered that six of the eight persons I had counseled and who turned out to have been demonized carried on active conversations with possessing demons. One twenty-five-year-old man, Allan, had been possessed from the age of five. His mother and grandmother practiced spiritualism. A being that called itself Justin came to him as a kind of playmate. At first Justin was fun and would comfort Allan when there was trouble at home or at school. Others became familiar with Justin but considered him just an imaginary playmate. But Justin became less and less fun as the years went by. He wanted Allan to do as he said, and when Allan wouldn't, Justine would punish him, usually through various fears. Justin even insisted that Allan commit suicide.

During my counseling with Allan, Justin would speak to me, argue vehemently at times, and refuse to budge from his home. He is gone now, though—cast out by Jesus. The demon was real, but the person he possessed was classified as a schizophrenic who spoke to unseen persons and heard voices. The voices, however, were real. Allan made several visits to mental hospitals and was usually treated with some kind of depressant, which only made it harder for him to resist Justin's orders.

June also heard voices. It led her to nine years of commitment to mental hospitals. June was a voice medium who gave predictions and prophecies. She thought she had been given a special gift from God, but over the years she was being robbed of her physical and emotional health. When she came to me for counseling, voices were continually speaking to her, urging her to discontinue the interviews. After several sessions we began to deal with the demons. They came out, one after another, six or seven of them; the voices disappeared. June still had emotional problems, but with the demons gone we were able to deal with the problems much more effectively.

If a demonized person is speaking to or hearing voices from unseen persons, the source or object of the communication is often identified as a guide spirit. Their spirit may even have a name. The instruction from such voices will be opposed to Jesus Christ, the Bible, and the Christian faith. These voices will often encourage a person to live morally and assert that it is not necessary to trust in God, read the Bible, or pray. The idea of forgiveness of sin is usually scoffed at. Doctor Lechler provides a helpful summary to this very complex problem.

> One can therefore say: a mentally ill person is in fact still ill, even when he exhibits certain symptoms characteristic of possession. On the other hand a possessed person is in fact

mentally healthy in spite of the fact that at intervals he may exhibit certain symptoms of mental abnormality. In addition to this it is noticeable that the mentally ill will usually give expression to their thoughts quite fervently, whereas, a possessed person will often do so only after much hesitations, and then only if he is urged to speak. While the mental patient will speak in extravagant tones of the demons he alleges to be living inside himself, the possessed person avoids all mention of demons as long as no one approaches him on a spiritual level. In this way the evil spirit prevents his victim from betraying his presence.[19]

Recently a neighbor asked me to visit her son, who was a patient in a mental health hospital. He had been deeply involved in Eastern religions, transcendental meditation, and organic foods (macrobiotics). He particularly liked to wear white or go without clothes altogether. He could enter into a passive or active state of mind at will. His psychiatrist was having no success with him, and medication was having little or no effect on him. When confronted with Jesus Christ, he became very aggravated and abusive. He would enter into a trance-like state of mind, in which an indwelling demon spoke and argued against the Bible and the Gospel. When the man was out of the trance, he was ignorant of the Bible, but while in the trance he demonstrated a great wealth of twisted Bible knowledge.

In counseling the demonized, there is usually considerable resistance to dealing with anything demonic or Christian, while the mentally ill may easily involve himself in either subject.

SUICIDE

There is usually a difference between a person prompted to suicide demonically and a person prompted to suicide as a result of mental depression and confusion. Satan's goal is to destroy life, especially if the death means that the person will be out of the reach of God. Death permanently separates the nonbeliever from God. A demonized person might experience direct and obvious promptings from the devil to kill himself, even to the point of choking himself to death. These

---

[19] Ibid, p. 162.

promptings are generally sudden and not the result of extreme mental depression. A mentally ill person is usually led to suicide after a growing period of depression and confusion. Such a depression can so alter the reason of the mentally ill that he is not actually responsible for his own actions.

Joan was a sixteen-year-old girl who had been involved in spiritualism. She had attempted séances even as a child. When she began to hear of Jesus, she experienced sudden, strong impulses to kill herself.

Another woman, having become demon-possessed through contact with palm readers, was witnessed to by some Christians. She strongly resisted the Gospel. Afterward, when driving her car, sudden thoughts came to her, urging her to speed up and crash into a truck. Only with great difficulty was she able to overcome these suicidal impulses.

BLASPHEMY

Blasphemy against God is common with both the mentally ill and the demonized. The blasphemous charges of the demonized do not usually make the person sorry or repentant; they are thoughts springing from the heart. The mentally ill generally experiences the blasphemous thoughts with regret or remorse. These thoughts of the mentally ill are experienced compulsively rather than as deep-seated attitudes. A longtime Satanist who operated a small satanic coffeehouse would loudly and viciously curse Jesus in the presence of Christians, but amid his own followers he would adopt a patronizing attitude toward the Lord.

PSYCHOPATHY

Psychopathy presents a rather difficult situation in that demonization and psychopathy often occur together so that the problems appear to be one and the same. It may be that the psycho-pathological personality is more vulnerable to being demonized than other forms of mental illness. But it is important to note that a person need not be mentally ill, in any way, to be demonized. One is not the cause or the effect of the other. It may be observed, though, that if the psycho-pathological person "expresses continual regret for his agitation, or dishonesty, or moodiness, one can immediately discard all thought of the demonic."[20]

It has been found that occasionally a person with a psychopathic personality may actually want to believe his problems result from demon possession. A new believer, thirty years old, with a past history of drug abuse, mental illness, and trouble with the police, attempted to persuade me that his only problem was demon possession. After a long counseling session, it was evident that there was no demonization; the problem was essentially psychological. To learn that a simple deliverance from demons was not the answer to his problems, the young man went into a temporary depression. He had been hoping for a quick remedy to his trouble.

EPILEPSY

Epilepsy is not a mental illness but seems to be basically a neurological problem. It has been attributed to demonic causes by some Christians. There is one instance in the New Testament where Jesus cast a demon out of a boy who the boy's father declared to be an epileptic (Matt. 17:15). Mark 9:17 and Luke 9:39 both say the boy had a spirit (an evil spirit). The boy suffered from fits that convulsed him, causing him to fall to the ground, which actually endangered his life, since he was prone to fall into fire or water. The fact that the convulsive fits often resulted in near death for the boy suggests the demonic nature of the fit. The demon was cast out of the boy by Jesus, and the boy was healed.

The demon may have expressed itself through an epileptic-type seizure. It is only by way of the father's report that the subject of epilepsy even enters the picture. One does not have to accept the father's evaluation as wholly accurate anymore than one must accept as true some of the statements that the Bible writers record Satan as making. Jesus Himself did not comment on the father's diagnosis—He simply ministered deliverance.

This view is further strengthened by the fact that medicines administered to known epileptics (epilepsy reveals characteristic brain wave patterns) have alleviated symptoms, and by the fact that Christians have had epilepsy and have manifested no demonic traits. Demons may cause symptoms in a person that take on the appearance

---

[20] Ibid, p. 185.

of epilepsy, but real cases of epilepsy are not the result of demons. This conclusion finds support in Matthew 4:24, where epileptics are classed separately from demoniacs.

THE PROBLEM OF PARAPSYCHOLOGY AND ESP

The word "parapsychology" means a study of phenomena that are related to psychology. Milan Ryzl defines parapsychology as "the study of phenomena not explainable by common energetic effects."[21] The "science" has much to do with extrasensory perception, though it generally holds that such perception is not actually "extra" but merely beyond what man has been acquainted with. ESP is generally considered the transmission of information effectuated by signals carried by some unknown kind of energy. Ryzl says, "ESP should be understood as a process analogous to sensory perception."[22]

I have included ESP in the occult field, although the question as to the place of ESP is debated by some Christians. It is the writer's feeling, based on considerable experience and research, that the whole range of the study of parapsychology is the occult. Parapsychology is not occult but rather the study of occult practices, while ESP is a label given to certain occult practices such as clairvoyance, clairaudience, telepathy, and the contacting of spirits.

One of the subfields of parapsychology is psychokinesis, which is the concept that man's mind (psyche) can influence the movement or actually cause the movement of material objects. But psychokinesis, or PK, again is a designation for demonic phenomena. PK, Ryzl says, resembles "ESP in all main characteristic features."[23]

ESP is observable and measurable scientifically. Again Ryzl says, "On the basis of the results of a number of quantitative experiments of the described type, we may say that the existence of extrasensory perception has been proved."[24] Spiritualists and other occultists have been saying this and trying to prove it for years, but with the investigations conducted at Duke University in Durham, North Carolina, and

---

[21] Milan Ryzl, *Parapsychology: A Scientific Approach* (New York; Hawthorn Books, Inc., 1970), p. 3.

[22] Ibid, p 11.

[23] Ibid, p. 164,

[24] Ibid, p. 75.

the establishment there of the Foundation for Research on the Nature of Man (FRNM), in 1964, and other centers, ESP has been amply demonstrated. There is no longer any real question about it. There is such a thing as ESP. Gertrude Schmeidler, an expert on ESP, has said, "The most important basic finding about ESP is that it occurs, that extrachance response to stimuli has been demonstrated under conditions that preclude sensing, remembering, or inferring the stimuli."[25]

THEORIES ON THE NATURE OF ESP

Parapsychologists differ as to what makes ESP work. J. B. Rhine, one of the major founders and leaders in the field of parapsychology, says that it is based on Psychic energy as opposed to straight physical causes. He is certain the experiments conducted at Duke University prove that "...physical energies are ruled out."[26] Rhine himself describes the working principle behind ESP to be what he calls "nonphysical energetics."

Ryzl, in his *Parapsychology: A Scientific Approach*, has classified various approaches to the understanding of ESP. They are:

1. ESP does not exist, and what we take for ESP are in fact artifacts of non-parapsychological origin.

2. ESP exists, but we interpret it incorrectly; it is not a "perception" in the usual sense of this word.

3. ESP exists; it is really a "perception" by some new sense, but it is explainable by principles known today to natural science.

4. ESP exists; it is a "perception," but it is not explainable by any combination of principles hitherto known to natural science.

These classifications do not begin to cover all the possible theories being advanced. In Ryzl's forth category, dozens of possible sources for the energies of ESP have been proposed. It has been thought that there exists realms of the dead, inhabited by deceased persons' spirits that can contact the living world; supracosmological beings that

---

[25] Gertrude Schmeidler, ed., *Extrasensory Perception* (New York: Atherton Press, 1969), p.10.

[26] J. B. Rhine, *Parapsychology: From Duke to FRNM* (Durham, N. C.: The Parapsychology Press, 1965), p. 32.

can participate in human affairs; a mind or minds that can reach into the phenomenological experience of man; untapped or undiscovered energies emanating from the mind or other glands in the human body; a negative or opposite counterpart to every sort of objective reality that may influence the objective reality. It seems doubtful whether science will arrive at a common explanation for ESP. However, biblical demonology provides a basis for the understanding of ESP.

Parapsychology measures real phenomena; ESP really is extra-sensory perception. The parapsychologist measures, probably without realizing it, effects that the demonic can cause. In the Bible Satan is referred to as the "god of this world" who works in a spiritual way and is able to alter natural law. It is not understood exactly how Satan works, but he works in a spiritual manner. The parapsychologist, then, when he analyzes and measures para-psychological phenomena, is actually encountering the demonic.

ALTERED OR PASSIVE STATE OF MIND

Before leaving the discussion of parapsychology, Ryzl points up something very interesting in regard to ESP. It concerns the altered or passive state of mind observed to take place among people who have made good ESP subjects. The altered state of mind is strangely similar to the trances and/or hypnotic states that spiritualist mediums or other occultists experience when they are involved in occult activities. Ryzl says:

> Without question, a somewhat altered state of mind is important for the manifestation of ESP. G. N. M. Tyrrell noted that for the manifestation of ESP a certain state is necessary—a slight departure from the normal state of consciousness—and this state is inhibited by the slightest degree of self-consciousness, discomfort, or mental or physical disturbance.[27]

Ryzl give the example of a Mr. de Fleuriere, who was a good ESP subject, especially as a clairvoyant:

> I am fully aware of the fact that the mental state I am in has nothing to do with my usual mental state. I am no more the

---

[27] Ryzl, op. cit., p. 103

same man; I do not see or feel in the same way as before. I feel I have a double personality or, rather, as if one other person hidden in my deeper interior had suddenly emerged and replaced my normal personality. But yet, it does not seem to me that my usual thinking is entirely destroyed, this is certainly not the case. But beneath the surface of my conscious intelligence which directs my usual life, I feel there lives and works a subconscious intelligence, which is faster and more comprehensive than this one.... When this state lasts somewhat longer, I literally feel absorbed in that peculiar state of elation that we experience, for example, when we feel fascinated by a musical or poetical inspiration. I experience it so strongly that I often entirely lose the awareness of the place where I am, and of the objects that interest me. I get into this state and out of it very quickly, almost as easily as when I open or close my eyes in order to get into or out of the contact with the outer world. After long sittings I feel in a state that decidedly is no less favorable for the manifestation of my ability, rather on the contrary. I feel my elation increase, and in parallel with its growth my mental exaltation is enhanced which increases my ability of paranormal perception.[28]

In addition, Ryzl cites the example of Mr. Frederik Marion:

Anybody can produce psychic phenomena, if he only can lose himself within himself. In other words, the mind, at such times, must strip off the veneer of normal materialistic habits and strive to reach a unity with something beyond time, space, and causality. There is no word entirely suitable for describing such a condition of the mind, and for lack of a more accurate term I must use the word, "concentration."[29]

Marion also reported how he received extrasensory information:

I establish a knowledge of the "feel" of the object. The word "feel" is inadequate, but I am compelled to use ordinary words

---

[28] Ibid, p. 104.
[29] Ibid.

to describe extra-ordinary sensations.... A touch, for me, gives thoroughly concrete impressions. They are really coherent, even if I am unable to describe them verbally. These impressions go further than form and condition, as they include a plus quality beyond the normal comprehension of our five senses... . A multitude of varied impressions connect with mundane surroundings [are coming]. Some are shutting out the disturbing factors and allowing the helpful impressions to stream into the conscious or subconscious in order to carry out the experiment successfully.[30]

Ryzl's discussion centers around the study of ESP and other parapsychological phenomena. I have noticed, however, that the altered state of mind is very much a part of the occult experience.

It has been a rather common experience in recent year to find middle class people becoming demon-possessed through such seemingly harmless practices as yoga meditation for weight-reducing and mind relaxing, mind growth or awareness exercises, tapping into "alpha wave levels," and mental exercises aimed at achieving positive or creative thinking that center around a passive, calm, clear or God-conscious state of mind. Or it may be that one particular object, idea, or thought is centered on.

A woman I interviewed had come under demonic influence through a mental awareness group that blanked all things out of their mind except the word "Jesus." One group advertises that through tapping into "alpha wave levels," the mind reaches a state of bliss, which helps the businessman cope with his problems. Businessmen pay large fees for the opportunity to expose themselves to the demonic through such mind awareness groups.

DISCUSSION QUESTIONS

1. How might the account of the Gerasene demoniac (Matt. 8:28–34; Mark 5:1–20; and Luke 8:26–39) be demythologized? What does this method of interpretation do to the authenticity of the Bible?

2. How might the account of the blind and dumb demoniac (Matt.

---

[30] Ibid, p. 105.

12:22–30; Mark 3:22–27; and Luke 11:14–23) be understood from an existential point of view? Could one existentialize the demonic and believe in its reality at the same time? Explain your answer.

3.   Examine each particular world view to see how it varies from the biblical view of demonology, and examine each view as to whether it is adequate to answer the problem that occult phenomena present in our society today.

4.   How can the age-old question, "How can God be good if He allows Satan and demons to be in the world" be answered? How does dualism conflict with the Bible?

5.   What biblical support can be found that demonstrates the distinction between disease and the demonic? What part dos the demonic play in regard to disease?

6.   How is ESP (clairvoyance, telepathy, etc.) contrary to the Bible? Why is it difficult to express clearly the anti-Christian character of ESP?

7.   The altered or passive state of mind is considered essential for ESP phenomena to occur. Why, in the light of biblical demonology, might this be true?

8.   Are there non-occult groups in your area that employ occult-related techniques? Tell what you can about them.

Fallen Cherub, to be weak is miserable,
Doing or suffering: but of this be sure—
To do aught good never will be our task,
But ever to do ill our sole delight,
As being the contrary to his high will
Whom we resist.

JOHN MILTON
Paradise Lost

3
Biblical Perspectives on Demonology

OLD TESTAMENT DEMONOLOGY

ORIGIN OF PAGAN DEMONOLOGY

A belief in demons goes back to the earliest times. The ancients did not always think alike about demons, but most believed in powers, beings, spirits, or demons that could influence the lives of men. The ancient literature of the peoples living around the eastern shore of the Mediterranean testifies to their belief in demons, gods and spirits.

Canaanite demonology. The civilization around the Israelite peoples, both prior to their exodus from Egypt and including their settling of the Canaanite territory, were peoples who had concepts of demonology. These concepts had some influence on the demonology of the Israelites, although the extent of this influence is difficult to ascertain.

Oesterley and Robinson write, "It is well known that Assyro-Babylonian demonology had a considerable influence on Jewish belief in demons."[1] The Persians seem to have influenced Israelite demonology, especially concerning astrology and fortune-telling. Also, popular Israelite belief in spirits and demons, according to Werner Foerster, was evidently very "similar to the popular Greek belief in spirits."[2] The

---

[1] W. O. E. Oesterley and Theodore H. Robinson, *Hebrew Religion, Its Origin and Development* (London: S. P. C. K., 1952), p. 116.

[2] Werner Foerster in *Theological Dictionary of the New Testament*, ed. Gerhard Kittel and trans. Geoffrey W. Bromiley (Grand Rapids: Wm. B. Eerdmans Publishing Co., 1964), vol. 2, p. 10.

people with whom the Israelites were associated paid a great deal of attention to demon-like beings. This could be seen in their practical as well as in their religious life.

Old Testament warnings about involvement with sorcery, sooth-saying, and similar practices testify that beliefs of some peoples influenced Israelite religion. Exodus 22:18 instructs that a sorceress was to be killed. Leviticus 19:26 warns against the practice of augury (a form of fortune-telling) and witchcraft. Verse 31 of that same chapter warns against consulting mediums or wizards, for such contact would bring defilement. Leviticus 20:6, 27 declares a strong judgment against a person seeking out a medium or wizard. Deuteronomy 4:19 warns against worship of stars; this applies to astrology. And Deuteronomy 18 has the most complete listing of occult practices to be found in the Old Testament:

> *"When you come into the land which the LORD you God gives you, you shall not learn to follow the abominable practices of those nations. There shall not be found among you...any one who practices divination, a soothsayer, or an augur, or a sorcer-er, or a charmer, or a medium, or a wizard, or a necromancer. For whoever does these things is an abomination to the LORD; and because of these abominable practices the LORD your God is driving them out before you. You shall be blameless before the LORD your God."[3]*

It is clear from this one passage that God stands directly against every major phase of the occult including magic, fortune-telling, and spiritualism.

2 Kings 21 relates the story of Manasseh, one of the most evil of the Judean kings. He was involved in several occult practices (v. 6), for which he was severely judged by God.[4] He was involved in soothsaying and augury, and he dealt with mediums and wizards. The mediums and wizards were particularly adept at controlling spirits and spiritual forces.

The Old Testament clearly prohibits the Israelites from

---

[3] Deuteronomy 18:9–13
[4] Other related passages are 2 Chronicles 33:1–12; Isaiah 2:6; 8:19; 47:12, 13; and Daniel 2:27.

involvement in pagan demonic practices. Thus, Jewish religion, insofar as it adhered to the truth of the Bible, remained free from occult evil. The pure monotheism of the Israelites kept pagan demonology from entering into orthodox religious faith and practice.

Some Hebrew people, however, were involved in pagan demonology; the prohibitions against such practices were often broken. For example, it was necessary for Saul to rid the land of necromancers.[5] Occultists were repressed, but they continued to influence the common people. Necromancy is found only on the margin of the Old Testament due to the prohibitions against any contact with spirits of the dead.

The lands about Israel were full of demonism, and much of it came from the Babylonians, Assyrians, Persians, and Arabs; yet the influences from sources were countered with prohibitions. Yehezk El Kaufmann says, "There is no link of nomenclature between Israelite demons and pagan divinities."[6] In addition, biblical prohibitions against demonism distill the pagan conceptions to a much simpler scheme than actually existed among the pagans. Pagan demonism was chaotic and complicated, and the biblical writers picked out the central elements in their demonology and presented them in an orderly manner when they spoke against them.

Foerster shows that post-exilic Judaism greatly broadened the concept of demons. Tannaitic Judaism used demonic ideas to explain sicknesses and bizarre events.[7] Later Judaistic writers taught that the study of the Torah and trust in God and His angels would protect one from demons. Foerster explains that Judaism did not see demons as intermediaries between God and man but as subordinates of Satan. Also, demons were considered to be evil. Yet the Jewish people — including both the Old Testament and the extra-canonical literature— had a purer demonology than was popularly held to by their pagan neighbors.

---

[5] Necromancy aims at contacting so-called spirits of the dead. Animistic concepts may lie behind necromancy. In animism it is held that men have spirits that survive the death of the body, and these departed spirits are capable of influencing the living.

[6] Yehezk El Kaufmann, *The Religion of Israel* (Chicago: The University of Chicago Press, 1960), p. 64.

[7] Foerster, op. cit., pp. 12–14.

Animistic Influences. The problem of the origin of pagan demonology remains. Oesterley and Robinson hold that the Old Testament demonology comes from earlier animistic conceptions. They contend that demonism developed from the idea that trees and other natural objects were inhabited by spirits. These spirits were gradually referred to as gods or demons. A summary statement of Oesterley and Robinson says, "At present we are concerned merely to show that the Old Testament itself gives indications that Hebrew religion passed through the Animistic stage of belief."[8] Their idea, then, is that a possible origin for Old Testament demonology lies in early animistic conceptions.

Merrill Unger disclaims this theory. He holds that the concept of demons coming from animism through polytheism to monotheism is erroneous. He feels that animism is a degradation from good religious faith and practice. Monotheism (a belief in one God) was the earliest form of religion; it gradually corrupted into polytheism (belief in plural gods), and at last sank into animism. Thus, Unger contends that there is in general a downward rather than an upward tendency in ethnic faiths. He has a helpful statement about the idea of biblical demonology developing from animism through polytheism to the monotheism of Israel.

> To make polytheism the source of Biblical demonology is indeed a bold step, contradicting the lofty spirit of the Old Testament which manifests how slight and unimportant was the pagan deities as demons in no wise proves that polytheism is the source of Biblical demonology. It would rather indicate the category of demons already well known to Hebrew thought, and that heathen idolatry was interpreted as initiated and energized by demonic activity and deception.[9]

Summary Statement. All the influences on Old Testament demonology are not clearly understood. But the ultimate source of demonological information is the revealed Word of God. There is a basic similarity between the Old Testament accounts of the demonic

---

[8] Oesterley and Robinson, op. cit., p. 26.
[9] Merrill F. Unger, *Biblical Demonology* (Wheaton, Ill.: Scripture Press, 1952), p. 13–14.

and the traditions of other ethnic faiths familiar to the Israelites; but the similarities point to a common source, with the Old Testament preserving the clearest and most accurate account of demonology.

As to the question of where demons come from, the Old Testament is largely silent. The Old Testament preserves the clearest and purest conceptions of demonology, particularly as seen in Moses' prohibitions, yet it would be unwise to insist on an origin for the demonology of the Old Testament outside of the Scripture itself. God reveals in the Bible the clearest picture of the demonic that the world has known.

PRINCIPLES BEHIND DEMONIC INCIDENTS IN THE OLD TESTAMENT

The Old Testament does not abound with material relating to demonology that is appropriate to this study. The story of the witch of Endor and various prohibitions against demonic practices comprise nearly all the relevant material. There are many passages bearing on demonology, especially in connection with names of Satan and names of strange beings and creatures that may have a reference to pagan deities (or demons), but they do not come under the range of this study. The aim here is to examine relevant incidents in order to determine principles concerning demonic practices. By getting to the principles behind demonic incidents, we can examine contemporary demonic activity from a biblical perspective.

Power and knowledge. Biblical prohibitions illustrate two principles of the demonic: (1) the desire to control supernatural power or spirits, and (2) the desire for knowledge that cannot be obtained through ordinary means. In Exodus, Leviticus, and Deuteronomy there are strong prohibitions against such practices as divination, soothsaying, augury, charming, wizardry, necromancy, consulting mediums, and sorcery.[10] People engaged in and encountering such practices were not necessarily temple priests or caretakers of pagan shrines. They were occult practitioners. Wizards, charmers, and sorcerers could provide protection against spirits or demons, or even cause some kind of physical effect such as disease or death. Essentially these

---

[10] Exodus 22:18; Leviticus 19:26, 31; 20:6, 27; and Deuteronomy 4:19, 18:9–12.

people were sources of spiritual power which they made available to a person seeking their services. So an important principle of demonology is revealed in Old Testament warnings and prohibitions—the direction and control of spiritual power. Such power was to be used for personal gain or advantage.

The diviners, soothsayers, mediums, necromancers, and augurs were people involved in fortune-telling. Their methods differed greatly, yet the desired end was always the same—foretelling or predicting future events. Right along with the wizards, charmers, and sorcerers, they were declared to be working against God and His people. A second principle of demonology is thus revealed, and that is a desire for knowledge, particularly of future events. It is a desire to know things that cannot be gained through ordinary, physical ways.

These practices are expressly stated to be evil in 2 Kings 21:6 and 2 Chronicles 33:6. Both passages refer to the reign of Manasseh, king of Judah, a particularly black period in the history of the nation. The same two principles of demonology found through a study of the Pentateuchal prohibitions are observed again in the evil practices of King Manasseh. It is said of him that "he burned his son as an offering, and practiced soothsaying and augury, and dealt with mediums and wizards. He did much evil in the sight of the Lord, provoking him to anger."[11] Manasseh was intent on controlling and directing spirit power (with the help of wizards and mediums) and was interested in knowing the future (with the help of soothsayers and augers).

Saul's encounter with the medium of Endor points up the principle of demonology having to do with the desire for knowledge. At one point in his reign Saul commanded that mediums and wizards be expelled from the land.[12] In desperation, however, Saul himself sought out a medium so that he could obtain certain information from her. Saul's servants found the person their master was looking for in a medium who lived in Endor. The king disguised himself and paid a visit to her at night. He asked her to bring Samuel, the great prophet, up from the dead. [13]

---

[11] 2 Kings 21:6

[12] 1 Samuel 28:3b. The entire account is found in 1 Samuel 28:3–25.

[13] There are striking differences between this incident and the spiritualist séance in which communication with the dead is assumed to be established.

Saul intended to get advice from Samuel concerning a course of action in the war against the Philistines. He wanted knowledge. Saul's desire and belief are typical of one wanting the service of an occultist. Saul evidently believed that it was possible to contact the spirit of a deceased person and that such a spirit could supply him with extraordinary knowledge.

The prophet Isaiah accused the people of Judah of trafficking with diviners and soothsayers. He declared that God had rejected them for such activity.[14] Isaiah believed God wanted His people to seek Him out, to trust and obey Him, and not to establish contact with occult practitioners. At another time Isaiah asked, "Should not a people consult their God?"[15]

Isaiah's taunt against the nation Babylon is the most revealing of all the words of his prophecy in regard to demonology. His taunt illustrates two principles of biblical demonology: the desire for power and the desire for knowledge:

Stand fast in your enchantments and your many sorceries, with which you have labored from your youth; perhaps you may be able to succeed, perhaps you may inspire terror. You are a wearied with you many counsels; let them stand forth and save you, those who divide the heavens, who gaze at the stars, who at the new moons predict what shall befall you. Behold, they are like

---

Joseph Bayly, in his book, *What About Horoscopes?* (Elgin, Illinois: David C. Cook Publishing Co., 1970), pp. 70–71, lists three important differences between Saul's encounter with the medium of Endor and communication with the spirits of dead persons that is supposed to occur in some spiritualist séances. (1) Saul recognized Samuel: he did not have to take the medium's word for it. (2) Samuel spoke like Samuel, and not out of the medium's mouth as in most spiritualist séances. (3) The medium was very frightened in this case in contrast to a spiritualist medium's séance. Such are Bayly's comments. A fourth distinction might be that the message Samuel gave to Saul was biblical in content and not contrary to the will or purpose of God. It may be concluded that the account of Samuel being brought up from the dead was an intervention by God: it was God's wording and not the result of a medium's work. God overruled the medium's work and acted so as to deal with King Saul.

[14] Isaiah 2:6
[15] Isaiah 8:19

stubble, the fire consumes them; they cannot deliver themselves
from the power of the flame. No coal for warming oneself is this,
no fire to sit before![16]

In verse 12 Isaiah accuses the Babylonians of clinging to their enchantments and sorceries in order that they might cause terror. It is not clear what is meant by enchantments, but sorcery is an attempt to control spiritual power. Sorcery is magic, and the desired result of it in the case of the Babylonians would be to inspire terror—the manipulation of spiritual power. In verse 13 Isaiah ridicules the Babylonian astrologers. Their function is to predict coming events, that is, they are fortune-tellers who base their predictions on astrological occurrences. The astrologers are after knowledge—knowledge of the future. Thus, the two general principles of demonology are revealed here: the desire to control or manipulate spiritual power, and the desire for knowledge through means beyond normal sensory perception.

Ezekiel 13:17–20 refers to magic bands, possibly amulets, that were used to "hunt for souls," The magic bands refer either to charms used to bring people under the control of others or to amulets used in contacting the dead. Ezekiel, then, was referring either to sorcerers or necromancers, but in either case the reason for the practice was to accomplish something through spiritual power. Hence is seen the idea of power associated with demonic practices.

In Genesis 3:1–7 the serpent (or Satan)[17] enticed Eve. He questioned her about the command of God: "but of the tree of the knowledge of good and evil you shall not eat, for in the day that you eat of it you shall die."[18] Eve had heard God's command, but the serpent challenged the command. He declared God was wrong about death resulting from eating of that particular tree. The serpent even suggested that God gave the command to keep Eve in a state of ignorance,

---

[16] Isaiah 47:12–14

[17] The text refers to a serpent and not to Satan. The serpent has often been identified with Satan by Bible commentators. The question is: if the serpent is not Satan or does not symbolically represent Satan, then who or what is the serpent? This writer identifies the serpent of Genesis 3 with the biblical Satan. The writer of Revelation seems to have identified Satan with a serpent (perhaps the serpent of Genesis 3) in Revelations 12:9 and 20:2.

[18] Genesis 2:17

not knowing good and evil. Eve was tempted to acquire knowledge of that which God did not want known.

Frustration of the will of God. Lying behind the principles of the demonic—the desire for power and knowledge—is another central purpose of Satan: the frustration or perversion of the will of God.

In Genesis 2:17 Adam and Eve had been instructed by God not to eat of the tree of the knowledge of good and evil. It was a clear prohibition. The Satanic serpent's intent was to countermand the express commandment of God; Satan sought to frustrate the will of God. In obeying Satan, Eve rebelled against God. Participation in the occult is simply spiritual rebellion. The prophet Samuel made this clear when he confronted Saul over the king's disobedience to an express command of God regarding war with the Amalekites. Samuel said to Saul: "For rebellion is as the sin of divination."[19]

NEW TESTAMENT DEMONOLOGY

SOURCES OF NEW TESTAMENT DEMONOLOGY

New Testament believers accepted the existence of demons. They had no special need to formulate a new demonology; they were heirs to an already developed one. What is difficult to ascertain, however, is the extent to which their "popular" theology of demonology was altered and corrected by Jesus' teaching and ministry and their own encounters with the demonic.

The attention given the demonic in the New Testament is not very extensive, but it is of a different type than that found in the Old Testament. Demonic material in the New Testament is more experiential in nature than we find earlier. Jesus encountered a number of demonized people and ministered to them, and the disciple likewise had to deal with cases of demonization. There are warnings and judgments given concerning the demonic in the New Testament, but not to the extent of the Old Testament.

The intertestamental period. During the intertestamental period, particularly the last two centuries before Christ, belief in the devil and evil spirits (gods or demons) became more widespread. A survey of intertestamental literature demonstrates that increasing attention

---

[19] 1 Samuel 15:23a

was given to the demonic.

The Jewish concept of the demonic grew rapidly, then, during that time. Possible sources of influence would have been the Egyptians, Persians, Greeks and the non-Jewish Semitic groups. The extent of the influence from other cultures is difficult to measure, but, by the New Testament period, there was a strong place for the demonic in Jewish thought. Jesus and His disciples were certainly a part of their Hebrew cultural and religious setting, yet the New Testament's description of the demonic varies significantly from popular notions.

The mystery religions. The mystery religions of Asia Minor were rife with belief in demons. They produced excessive superstition and fear in the adherents. These religious teachings had a widespread effect upon the New Testament world.

William Fairweather, in his discussion of the mystery religions, says,

> If the Mysteries erred in entangling themselves with astral-
> ism, they erred still more in allying themselves to magic. The
> desire of Simon Magus to purchase from the Apostles the
> power of performing miracles in consequence of the teaching
> of Paul (Acts 19:19), illustrates the extent to which the black
> art was practiced in Asia Minor. Magic and the Mysteries were
> in great demand as a means of supposed deliverance from the
> malice of demons, "the slings and arrows of outrageous for-
> tune," and the rigours of Fate.[20]

It would have been nearly impossible to live in Palestine in the first century and be oblivious to the ideas of demons through the influence of the mystery religions. Even Galilee would not have pro-vided sufficient insulation from these doctrines and practices.

Persian and other influences. Along with the mystery religions there were other Persian or Iranian influences upon Jewish demon-ology. During the post-exilic and intertestamental periods, the con-ception of demons, as of angels, was greatly influenced by Persian thought. The actual extent of the Persian influence is not easy to mea-sure; however, there are differences between Jewish notions of the

---

[20] William Fairweather, *The Background of the Epistles* (Edinburgh: T. and T. Clark, 1935), p. 270.

demonic and the notions of the Persians and others. In regard to the Persian influence, Unger writes, "Israel's monotheism, moreover, kept its demonism singularly uncontaminated from a threatening dualism."[21] Yet Unger also points out that by the time of the ministry of Jesus, even popular Jewish demonology had badly deteriorated into a system of almost incredible and fanciful superstitions, contrasting with both the Old and New Testament.

It is clear, then, that Jewish popular conceptions of demonology showed significant affinity to the influences coming from the Egyptian mystery religions, the Persian dualistic beliefs, and other Semitic religions. Yet the official religion of the Jews was not so greatly touched.

Rabbinic Judaism. In regard to rabbinic Judaism and its influence on New Testament demonology, the opinion of scholars is divided. Some feel New Testament demonology is quite similar to that of the rabbis; others maintain they are highly dissimilar.

Merrill Unger describes the rabbinical ideas of demons as very crude and unbiblical, He acknowledges similarities of form between rabbinic Judaism's demonology and the New Testament, but he is very emphatic about the differences. He says, "Greater antithesis could scarcely be imagined than there is between the elevated tone of New Testament demonology and the crude views and practices mentioned in the Rabbinic writings."[22]

So there is a division of opinion in regard to rabbinic Judaism's influence on New Testament demonology, as there are conflicts of opinion regarding Persian influences. Essentially, the difference lies in the way the New Testament treats the demonic. It acknowledges the satanic, yet Jesus and His followers are never in fear of the demons or reduced to superstitious practices in defending against them. Satan is not the equal of God, and the individual in Christ has victory and freedom over Satan.

However, rabbinic literature does present two classes of inferior beings in the spiritual world—angels and demons. But the angels never possess a person, while demons may. Such a possession is in opposition to Holy Spirit possession. A demon was often referred to as an unclean sprit. The origin of demons was occasionally traced

---

[21] Unger, op. cit., p. 26.

[22] Ibid, p. 34

back to the passage in Genesis 6:1–4 according to Jubilees 10:1–16 and Enoch 15 and 16. Zucker writes that the demons were said to "be children of the fallen angels to whom the mysterious archaic passage of Genesis 6:1–4 seemed to refer."[23] Also, rabbis taught that the main function of the demons was to cause people harm (physical and economic). Those who followed such demons became demonic themselves.

It appears that some similarities may be found between the demonologies of rabbinical Judaism and the New Testament , but the demonology of the later is purer than others and heir to the generally lofty view of the demonology of the religion of Israel as chiefly expressed in the Old Testament.

In addition to the influence of the mystery religions, the Persians, and rabbinic Judaism on New Testament demonology, it is necessary to examine the ideas of the Greeks. Hellenistic influences must be considered since the Greek language of that day is the language of the New Testament.

Greek influence. Foerster's work is particularly helpful at this point. He suggests that to get at the meaning of *daimon* one must look to animism as the popular background of Greek demonology. He concludes on that basis that the term *daimon* was used to define a major or minor deity It was a term applied to supernatural beings or supernatural power. Yet Foerster maintains that "The etymology of *daimon* is uncertain."[24] The term was also used in the Hellenistic world to define a power overtaking a man, a power that was potentially either harmful or helpful.

The popular religions of the Greeks used the word "demon" to describe intermediary beings existing and acting somewhere between the "gods" and men. It was theses intermediating beings who had contact with earthbound men, so that eventually the demons came to be seen as evil (matter being viewed as evil). Such demons were said to be capable of possessing men. Magic was used by the Greeks to control them.

---

[23] W. M. Zucker, "Demonic; From Aeschylus to Tillich," Theology Today 26 (April 1969), p. 40.

[24] Foerster, op. cit., pp. 1–2. In this study, all Greek New Testament words will appear in the transliterated form, that is, the Greek letters being replaced by their equivalent English letters.

Foerster provides the following summary of Greek demonology:

> In sum, we may say that in popular Greek belief the demon is
> a being, often thought of as a spirit of the dead, endowed with
> supernatural powers, capricious and incalculable, present in
> unusual places at particular times and at work in terrifying
> events in nature and human life, but placated, controlled or at
> least held off by magical means.[25]

Unger's discussion of the development and meaning of the term
daimon is very similar to Foerster's. Unger concludes with this para-
graph on the New Testament meaning of the term.

> From Homer down to New Testament times the sense of the
> *daimon* and *daimonion* is seen thus to have increased gradu-
> ally in its inferiority to *theos*,[26] and to have gathered round it
> more and more the sense of evil, until it reached its precise
> and invariable New Testament meaning of an "evil spirit" or
> "messenger and minister of the devil." As a spiritual being,
> demons are intelligent, vicious, unclean, with power to afflict
> man with physical hurt, and moral and spiritual contamina-
> tion.[27]

Thus, the Greek term daimon was appropriate for New Testament
usage, but the New Testament view of demons differed from the popular Greek understanding of demons.

Summary statement. Origins for demonology of the New Testament do not lend themselves to simple definition. The origin is complex at best, and similarities between the demonology of the New Testament and other cultural and religious views of demons may even
be misleading. It is helpful to note that the New Testament itself does
not directly discuss the origin of demons, although their existence is
clearly assumed.

---

[25] Ibid, p. 8.

[26] Transliterated from the Greek, translated "God" in the New Testament.

[27] Unger, op. cit., p. 61.

PRINCIPLES BEHIND DEMONIC INCIDENTS IN THE NEW TESTAMENT

Even though the New Testament contains more definite demonic incidents than does the Old Testament, few of these incidents are appropriate to this study. This section is concerned with the motivation in demonic incidents, the dynamics behind the scene. As in the discussion of the Old Testament material, there will be no attempt to exegete all the New Testament incidents concerning the demonic. Various incidents will be examined with a view toward uncovering the purposes behind them. Once these purposes are established, they become useful tools in examining contemporary demonology.

Knowledge. There are two important incidents in the Book of Acts that lend themselves to an examination of the principles of demonology. In Acts 16:16–18, Paul encounters a girl who, the writer of Acts says, had been demonized by a "spirit of divination." In this incident, the principle of desiring knowledge through means beyond the ordinary is illustrated. Paul, Silas, and others were involved in ministry in the Macedonian city of Philippi. The group were on their way to prayer when a girl, a slave of some soothsayers, began following the Christians and loudly calling out, "These men are servants of the Most High God, who proclaim to you the way of salvation" (v. 17). It is interesting to note that the girl accurately understood who Paul was and the meaning of his mission.

The girl is said to have had a spirit of divination, *puthona* or *puthona* as it is transliterated from the Greek. Originally the term referred to a serpent or dragon that guarded the Delphic oracle, but it later came to indicate divination or prophesy. In addition, it was used to describe a ventriloquist, who was said to have such a spirit in his belly. The girl was a slave of some soothsayers (diviners or fortune-tellers) and was used for the purpose of fortune-telling. The word for soothsayer, transliterated *manteuomene*, has nearly meaning as *puthona* (divination).

The slave followed the missionaries for days until finally Paul had had enough. The apostle was so annoyed at the situation that he turned to confront her. He did not address the girl directly, but rather the spirit (spirit of divination or fortune-telling) that indwelt her. He said to the spirit, "I charge you in the name of Jesus Christ to come out of her" (v. 18). The spirit came out.

An important connection between the occult and demons is seen in the passage. The girl was demonized (a spirit or demon was in her), and by the agency of help of the spirit she could foretell the future. It is clear there was a spirit, a spirit of divination or fortune-telling, indwelling the girl; she was demonized to the point of possession. After the spirit of divination was cast out, she could no longer foretell the future. Her owners quickly realized the change and saw they could no longer use her for financial gain.

A principle of the demonic becomes apparent in this incident— the desire for knowledge not available through any ordinary physical means. The demonic spirit apparently enabled the girl to know the future in some way. People wanting knowledge, essentially knowledge of the future, would come to her hoping to obtain it. The end point of many occult practices—such as soothsaying, fortune-telling, palmistry, an card reading—all involve the same principle of the demonic, the desire to know the future, the desire for supernatural knowledge.

Power. Acts 19:13–19 relates a different sort of demonic incident. It illustrates the principle of seeking for power through manipulation of spirits of spiritual power. While he was in Ephesus Paul and his company encountered a band of traveling Jewish exorcists. These exorcists were using the name of Jesus as a magic word or as a part of a magic formula to cast evil spirits out of demonized persons. Parallels to such a practice may commonly be found in contemporary magic and spiritualism.

The term translated "exorcist" in Acts 19:13a in most English translations is the Greek word transliterated *exorkizo*. It is used in Acts 19 and once in Matthew 26:63. In Matthew it is found on the lips of the high priest who, at the trial of Jesus, says, "I adjure you by the living God, tell us if you are the Christ, the Son of God."

In addition, in the latter part of Acts 19:13, a Jewish exorcist is quoted as saying to persons who were demonized, "I adjure you by the Jesus whom Paul preaches." The word "adjure" in this instance is the translation of *horkizo*, from which the word *exorkizo* is derived. *Horkizo* is used only twice in the New Testament. It is found in Mark 5:7, and it is used once by the exorcists as recorded in Acts 19:13b. In Mark the word is spoken by a demon that panics at the presence of Jesus. The demon says, "I adjure you by God, do not torment me." Then in 1 Thessalonians 5:27, Paul uses a form of the word *horkizo*.

Paul's word *enorkizo* is usually translated "charge" or adjure." Paul employed the word as part of a final exhortation to the believers in Thessalonica. This is the only time a form of the word *horkizo* is found on the lips of a Christian in the New Testament.

Neither *exorkizo* nor *horkizo* is used to describe a Christian casting out demons. Essentially, the term is a word commonly used in magical contexts, especially as part of an oath in magic rituals. An exorcist is an occultist. It is interesting to note that the high priest in Matthew 26:63, the demon in Mark 5:7, and the Jewish exorcists in Acts 19:13 all bring the name of deity into their magic oath. Paul also used the name of deity in 1 Thessalonians 5:27, but more in the sense of an exhortation or an encouragement. The Jewish exorcists of Acts 19 were actually involved in an occult activity, the attempt to use or control supernatural power for their own purpose. Possibly they had observed disciples like Paul being successful in bringing deliverance to the demonized through Jesus. The exorcists might then have been attempting to imitate the Christians' success by using the name of Jesus as part of a magical formula. However, they had not placed their faith in Christ; they had not experienced the new birth. Rather, they were outsiders who were hoping to control the spiritual power they assumed was associated with the name of Jesus. Again an important principle of the demonic comes to light, the desire to control or manipulate supernatural power.

It is interesting to note that the Jewish exorcists were able to contact the evil spirit in the demonized person, but they were unsuccessful in their attempt to cast it out. The man demonized by the evil spirit overpowered the exorcists (perhaps with the help of demonic power) and publicly disgraced them. The whole incident had such a telling effect that a great many occultists who had become believed confessed their error and publicly burned their books on the magical arts (Acts 19:19).

In the Book of Revelation there are four references to sorcerers: 9:21; 18:23; 21:8; and 22:15. Sorcery is in itself an attempt to manipulate spiritual power or spirits, so that a simple look at the word as used in the Book of Revelation may serve to illustrate a principle of demonology. In three of the cases the sorcerers are judged in association with murderers, the immoral, and idolaters.[28] In Revelation 9:21 the word is *pharmakeia*, meaning sorcery or magic.[29] In Revelation 21:8, the word is *pharmakeus*, meaning a magician or mixer of poisons. In Revelation 22:15 the word is *pharmakos*, meaning a magician or poisoner. The term carries the idea of sorcery or magic that uses charms and/or drugs. It is very clear that such sorcerers are against God and will receive just punishment in hell because of their practices. Revelation 21:8 describes the fate of the sorcerer in clear terms:

> But as for the cowardly, the faithless, the polluted, as for the murderers, fornicators, sorcerers, idolaters, and all liars, their lot shall be in the lake that burns with fire and sulphur, which is the second death.

The sorcerer, whether he is using drugs (or potions), charms, or other tools or fetishes, adequately portrays a central principle of the demonic—the seeking or desire to control or manipulate spiritual power or spirits. It is a desire to have power to use for personal gain or convenience.

The ministry of Jesus to the demonized. No reference has yet been made in this chapter to Jesus' ministry to the demonized. In the Synoptic Gospels there are six instances in which Jesus encountered demonized persons. They are:

1. the man with an unclean spirit at a synagogue in Capernaum—Mark 1:21–28 and Luke 4:31–37;

2. the blind and dumb demoniac—Matthew 12:22–29; Mark 3:22–27; and Luke 11:14–22;

3. the Gerasenes demoniac—Matthew 8:28–34; Mark 5:1–20; and Luke 8:26–39;

4. the Syrophoenician woman's daughter—Matthew 15:21–28 and Mark 7:24–30;

5. the epileptic boy—Matthew 17:14–21; Mark 9:14–29; and Luke 9:37–43a;

---

[28] In Revelation 18:23 the term "sorcerer" is used, but in a context that does not lend itself to this study.

[29] This is the word Paul uses in Galatians 5:20, translated "sorcery" in some and "witchcraft" in other translations.

6.   the woman with a spirit of infirmity—Luke 13:10–17.

There are also statements describing the types of ministry Jesus performed to the demonized. These passages are Matthew 4:24; 8:16; Mark 1:32–34; 1:39; 3:11; 6:13; and Luke 4:41; 6:18; 7:21. Mark 1:39 serves as an example of such passages. It reads, "And he went throughout all Galilee, preaching in their synagogues and casting out demons." Jesus' ministry to the demonized was not limited to just the six specific incidents recorded in the Synoptic Gospels. Since there are no instances in John's gospel of Jesus encountering demonized person, information regarding this ministry must be gleaned from the six stories in the Synoptic.

In Mark 1:21–28 and Luke 4:31–37 is found the account of the man with an unclean spirit whom Jesus met in a synagogue in Capernaum. Both Mark and Luke say that the man had an unclean spirit and that the spirit or spirits recognized Jesus as the "Holy One of God." It seems that Mark and Luke refer to one spirit, while the demon in speaking to Jesus said "us" at one point and "I" at another. Jesus, in ministering to the man, cast out only one demon. At the point of the expulsion, Mark says, the demon convulsed the man; Luke say the demon threw the man down. Jesus rebuked it, ordering it to be silent and come out. After the demon had come out, the observers were amazed that Jesus actually had such authority. It must have been obvious to the observers that a demon had indeed been cast out.

A second story is that of the blind and dumb demonized recorded in Matthew 12:22–29 and Luke 11:14–22. Mark 3:22–27 contains part of the story but does not describe Jesus' ministry to a demonized person. All three passages contain both the accusation against Jesus that He had cast out demons by Beelzebul and Jesus' reply that Satan does not cast himself out. Mark has the accusation narrative in a different context than Matthew and Luke. Matthew's account has the blind and dumb demoniac being brought to Jesus; Luke only mentions that the man was speechless and does not relate how Jesus and the demoniac met. Matthew says Jesus healed the demoniac while Luke says Jesus cast a demon out of the man. Both Evangelists describe the cure appropriately: Matthew's demoniac is able to speak and see, and Luke mentions only the dumb man could speak. The casting out of the demon was observed by various people, and when the Pharisees heard of the cure they accused Jesus face to face, arguing that His authority and power were from Beelzebul, prince of demons.

A third story concerns the Gadarene demoniacs or Gerasene demoniac. The story is recorded in Matthew 8:28–34; Mark 5:1–20; and Luke 8:26–39. Matthew says there were two persons, Mark and Luke mention only one of the two. Jesus met the demoniac in open country near the Sea of Galilee. Mark says the demoniac ran up to Jesus, having seen Him from afar, and worshiped Him; the man recognized Jesus as the "Son of the Most High God." It is not clear who was speaking, the demoniac or the demons, in regard to recognizing Jesus. In the request to be sent into the swine, it appears the demons (the legion) themselves were speaking. It seems Jesus addressed the man in asking for a name, but according to Mark it appears the legion (the demons) responded to the question using a plural personal pronoun. "we." Matthew does not record that Jesus asked for a name, and Luke edits the response to the legion by merely reporting the results.

This is the only incident recorded in which Jesus sought to know the name of a demon. It was assumed during New Testament times that, by knowing the name of a demon, an exorcist gained power over it. The reason for Jesus' desire to learn the names of the demons is not clear. Jesus did not cast the demons out but allowed the demons to leave as they had requested. The legion asked to enter into some swine that were feeding some distance away on a hillside. Jesus submitted to the request. The legion apparently entered the swine, thereby causing the whole herd to rush off a cliff to perish in the sea. This is a singular account and the only one like it in the Bible. The passages do not explain the occurrence: they just report it.

In Matthew 12:43–45 and Luke 11:24–26 Jesus speaks to wandering unclean spirits or demons. Luke 11:24–26 reads:

> *"When the unclean spirit has gone out of a man, he passes through waterless places seeking rest; and finding none he says, 'I will return to the house from which I came.' And when he comes he finds it swept and put in order. Then he goes and brings seven other spirits more evil than himself, and they enter and dwell there; and the last state of that man becomes worse than the first."*

Matthew records the saying also, but adds the comment, "So shall it be also with this evil generation" (12:45). It may be that the statement belongs to Matthew and not to Jesus. However, the story might give a clue as to why the demons desired to enter the swine after being cast out of the man. Demons desire to indwell a body—a flesh and bloody body—for the purpose of "rest." It seems unwise to draw any particular conclusions as to exactly why the demons wanted to enter the swine. Neither is it clear why the swine bolted over the cliff, except that the entrance of the demons into them seems to have been the immediate cause.

Mark and Luke record the transformation of the demoniac. People who had known the troubled man living among the tombs had no difficulty acknowledging the change. They further recognized that Jesus had been responsible for the man's transformation. Jesus was asked to leave the area.

Jesus was confident about the good results of His ministry to the demoniac; He requested that the man preach goodness of God to his friends.

A fourth incident is found in Matthew 15:21–28 and Mark 7:24–30, the story of the Syrophoenician woman's daughter. While travelling about the region of Tyre and Sidon, Jesus was sought out by a native of the area, a non-Jew, who reported explicitly that her daughter was demonized. After dealing with the woman's non-Jewishness, Jesus healed her daughter from a distance; the girl was not present with Jesus and her mother. In Mark's account, Jesus affirmed it was a demon that had been causing the trouble. Matthew simply records Jesus as saying, "O woman, great is your faith! Be it done for you as you desire" (v.28). Matthew states that the healing (or casting out of the demon) took place instantly, and Mark says the woman, upon arriving home, found her daughter well.

A fifth story, the account of the epileptic boy, is in Matthew 17:14–21; Mark 9:14–29; and Luke 9:37–43a. The story is misnamed, since it appears that the boy was not epileptic but demonized. In Matthew, the father stated his son was epileptic, Jesus did not confirm the father's diagnosis. Mark and Luke record the father as saying his boy had a "dumb spirit" (Mark 9:17) and a "spirit" (Luke (9:39). The father sought out Jesus after His disciples had failed to deal with the boy's problem. Mark states the spirit or demon recognized Jesus, "saw him," and began to convulse the boy so that he fell to the ground. Jesus rebuked the demon and ordered it to leave, never (according to Mark) to enter the boy again. The demon, according to Jesus, had entered or indwelt the boy. After a terrible struggle the demon came out, leaving the boy appearing more dead than alive. Jesus, however, helped the boy up, completing His ministry to him. When the disciples asked Him about their failure to solve the problem, Jesus attributed it to a lack of faith (according to Matthew) and a lack of prayer (according to Mark). Luke records that the eyewitnesses to the incident were astonished— astonished perhaps at the demon's obedience to the command of Christ.

A sixth story, found in Luke 13:10–17, concerns a woman who had a spirit of infirmity. Jesus was teaching in a synagogue, and one of the people there was a woman who for eighteen years had been bent over so that she could not fully straighten up. Jesus approached her directly and declared her to be freed from her illness. Even though Luke refers to a "spirit of infirmity," Jesus used the term "infirmity," indicating a physical rather than a demonic problem. Jesus then laid his hands on her, a typical Jewish custom in regard to healing, and she was made straight and began to praise God. The cure was immediate. It is thought that the incident involved a demon because of Jesus' statement in verse 16: "And ought not this woman, a daughter of Abraham whom Satan bound for eighteen years, be loosed from this bond on the Sabbath day?"

Coupling Luke's term "spirit of infirmity" with Jesus' reference to Satan, it seems that demonization was the woman's problem rather than a physical illness. If it was a case of demonization, it outwardly appeared physical in nature.

As this section on Jesus' ministry to the demonized concludes, it is doubtful any clear-cut principles of demonology emerge. Certainly the demonized were not experiencing a not experiencing a normal, healthy life. In that sense, demons had frustrated or perverted God's purpose for men's lives. Of course, many if not all present states of human existence are contrary to God's will. Demonic activity is not necessary for a frustration of the will of God. It is true that the demonic accounts alone are not used by the gospel writers to teach that the states of demonization frustrated the will of God. Such a conclusion would be reading into the texts that which is not obviously there. However, the demonization of a person is a frustration of God's will.

Frustration of the will of God. Demons seek to confuse and deceive believers doctrinally, thus perverting or frustrating the intent of God. Paul writes in 1 Timothy 4:1–3:

Now the Spirit expressly says that in later times some will depart from the faith by giving heed to deceitful spirits and doctrines of demons, through the pretensions of liars whose consciences are seared, who forbid marriage and enjoin abstinence from food which God created to be received with thanksgiving by those who believe and know the truth.

The doctrinal deviation Paul describes, the forbidding of marriage and abstaining from eating certain foods, are clearly perversions of the will of God, who established marriage and created all foods to be eaten. Spirts and demons are accused by Paul of activity whose purpose is to deceive men, to actually lead men to act contrary to the will of God in regard to marriage and food. Paul speaks of such doctrinal perversions as occurring in the "later times"; that is, just before the end of history, Satan will be especially active. This passage takes on new meaning as an occult revival is coming at a time when many Christians are looking for Jesus' second coming.

Paul's words in 2 Corinthians 4:4 also illustrate this third principle of demonology, the demonic's attempt to frustrate or pervert the intent, purpose, and will of God. Paul writes concerning those who rejected the Gospel of Christ: "In their case the god of this world has blinded the minds of the unbelievers, to keep them from seeing the light of the gospel of the glory of Christ, who is the likeness of God." Satan clearly wants people to miss the truth of God. He'll do it crudely or subtly, but he hates God's will to be worked out in anyone's life.

In Acts 13:6–12 there is the story of Paul's encounter with the magician, a Jewish false prophet named Bar-Jesus, or Elymas. Paul and Barnabas had just set off on the first missionary journey, and while they were on the island of Paphos they were asked by a Roman proconsul, Sergius Paulus, to speak to him concerning the Word of God. But Bar-Jesus, the magician, making it difficult for Paul to bear an effective witness, hoping to prevent Sergius Paulus from conversing at all with the apostle. Paul was annoyed at the magician and openly confronted him, saying, "You son of the devil, you enemy of all righteousness, full of all deceit and villainy, will you not stop making crooked the straight paths of the Lord?" (v.10). The magician was accused of being opposed to God. The occultist, Bar-Jesus, was being used of Satan to frustrate the preaching of Paul and thereby was involved in fighting against God.

The third principle can be demonstrated by yet another passage. The temptation of Jesus by Satan (Matthew 4:1–11; Mark 1:12–13; and Luke 4:1–13), particularly the first two challenges, show the satanic attempt to divert Christ from His intended ministry.

Satan wanted Jesus first to use His power to turn stones into loaves of b read. The Lord's reply to this temptation indicates that such an act was contrary to His own intention. Secondly, Satan wanted Jesus to throw Himself down from the pinnacle or high point of the Temple and thus through angelic intervention demonstrate great spiritual power (or perhaps cause Jesus' death in a way that was not intended by God). These two temptations were satanic attempts to frustrate the purpose of Christ. But thirdly, Satan wanted Jesus to worship him. This brings out a fourth principle of demonology: Satan worship.

Satan worship. The fourth biblical principle is illustrated by the third temptation, when Satan tempted Jesus to worship him. The principle is Satan worship.

Satan wants man to worship him. The end point of all the occult is Satan worship, either disguised or actual. In most forms of the occult, Satan is seriously avoided, but he is worshiped nevertheless, since contact with demons is nothing less than contact with Satan. Satan wants to be worshiped, and the occult arts are direct means of doing so. The astrologer, for example, would not like to believe himself to be the Satan worshiper that he actually is. Paul in 1 Corinthians 10:19, 20 says:

> What do I imply then? That food offered to idols is anything, or that an idol is anything? No, I imply that what pagans sacrifice they offer to demons and not to God. I do not want you to be partners with demons.

Even idolatry, because of the demonic involvement, is actually a worship of the demonic.

Summary statement. The purpose of this chapter to this point has been twofold. First, it has been to look at demonic influences current in Old and New Testament times, and second, to formulate basic principles of demonology based on the biblical material. The four principles of demonology outlined here will be used as tools for understanding contemporary demonology or occult practices.

THE ORIGIN AND NATURE OF DEMONS

THE ORIGIN OF DEMONS

Neither the Old nor the New Testament indicates precisely the origin of demons. The existence of demons and the devil is assumed by the biblical writers; however, Christians in both ancient and modern times have speculated about those origins. Many have asserted that the Bible clearly outlines the origin of demons as well as the origin of Satan. This assertion relies on certain biblical passages that seem to portray Satan as a fallen angel, an angel that rebelled against God and consequently was cast out of heaven; and thus the demons would also be angels, who followed Satan in his rebellion against God and suffered a like fate. This is a very reasonable explanation of the origin of both Satan and demons. Merrill Unger has written,

> Sin itself began in heaven with "Lucifer, son of the morning," the highest and most exalted of heaven's created beings, who became Satan when he led a celestial revolt that spread to myriads of the angelic beings.[30]

Origin of demons in the Old Testament. Unger refers to Isaiah 14:12–20 to support his contention that Satan is a fallen angel. This significant passage reads:

> How art thou fallen from heaven, O Lucifer, son of the morning! how art thou cut down to the ground, which didst weaken the nations! For thou hast said in thine heart, I will ascend into heaven, I will exalt my throne above the stars of God: I will sit also upon the mount of the congregation, in the sides of the north: I will ascend above the heights of the clouds; I will be like the most High. Yet thou shalt be brought down to hell, to the sides of the pit. They that see thee shall narrowly look upon thee, and consider thee, saying, Is this the man that made the earth to tremble, that did shake kingdoms; that made the world as a wilderness, and destroyed the cities thereof; that opened

---

[30] Unger, op. cit., p. 15.

not the house of his prisoners? All the kings of the nations, even all of them, lie in glory, every one in his own house. But thou art cast out of thy grave like an abominable branch, and as the raiment of those that are slain, thrust through with a sword, that go down to the stones of the pit; as a carcass trodden under feet. Thou shalt not be joined with them in burial, because thou hast destroyed thy land, and slain thy people: the seed of evildoers shall never be renowned. (KJV)

Although this passage refers primarily to the king of Babylon (Isaiah 14:3, 4, 22), it is obvious that there is a deeper meaning. In verse 12 Isaiah speaks of "Lucifer, son of the morning" as a being who has "fallen from heaven." Then the prophet gives the reason for Lucifer's fall: he has said, "I will ascend into heaven, ...I will be like the most High." Satan, at some time in the distant past, revolted against God and attempted to displace Him as the ruler of the universe. This willful act of rebellion caused him to be cast out of heaven.

Ezekiel 28:11¬–19 is another passage that may be viewed as referring to the origin of Satan. The passage reads:

Moreover the word of the LORD came unto me, saying, Son of man, take up a lamentation upon the king of Tyrus, and say unto him, Thus saith the Lord GOD; Thou sealest up the sum, full of wisdom, and perfect in beauty. Thou hast been in Eden the garden of God; every precious stone was thy covering, the sardius, topaz, and the diamond, the beryl, the onyx, and the jasper, the sapphire, the emerald, and the carbuncle, and gold: the workmanship of thy tabrets and of thy pipes was prepared in thee in the day that thou wast created. Thou art the anointed cherub that covereth; and I have set thee so: thou wast upon the holy mountain of God; thou hast walked up and down in the midst of the stones of fire. Thou wast perfect in thy ways from the day that thou wast created, till iniquity was found in thee. By the multitude of thy merchandise they have filled the midst of thee with violence, and thou hast sinned: therefore I will cast thee as profane out of the mountain of God: and I will destroy thee, O covering cherub, from the midst of the stones of fire. Thine heart was lifted up because of thy beauty, thou hast corrupted thy wisdom by reason of thy brightness: I will cast thee to the ground, I will lay thee before kings, that they may behold thee. Thou hast defiled thy sanctuaries by the multitude of thine iniquities, by the iniquity of thy traffick; therefore will I bring forth a fire from the midst of thee, it shall devour thee, and I will bring thee to ashes upon the earth in the sight of all them that behold thee. All they that know thee among the people shall be astonished at thee: thou shalt be a terror, and never shalt thou be any more. (KJV)

Some have felt this passage refers only to the king of Tyre, but this view is clearly wrong. There are three primary reasons to believe that these verses speak of Satan. First, verse 2 of the chapter speaks of the "prince of Tyrus," while verse 12 refers to the "king of Tyrus." There was no co-regency at this time. Tyre had only a king—there was no ruling prince. Obviously, the "prince of Tyrus" speaks of the man ruling over Tyre, while the "king of Tyrus" refers to the power behind the throne—Satan. Daniel 10:13, 20, 21 speaks of demonic forces ruling over nations in this way. Second, Ezekiel 28:13 declares, "Thou hast been in Eden." The king of Tyrus never could meet this qualification. Third, verse 14 speaks of him as the "anointed cherub." Taken objectively, this passage of Scripture clearly pictures Satan, the power behind the throne of Tyrus, as one who sinned and was cast "out of the mountain of God" (v.16).

Origin of demons in the New Testament. Two New Testament passages sometimes used to prove an origin for demons are 2 Peter 2:4 and Jude 6. The verse in 2 Peter reads, "For if God did not spare the angels when they sinned, but cast them into hell and committed them to pits of nether gloom to be kept until the judgment; ..." And Jude 6 says, "And the angels that did not keep their own position but left their proper dwelling have been kept by him in eternal chains in the nether gloom until the judgment of the great day...."

Both passages refer to angels who had sinned or had left their proper dwelling place and had been cast into hell to be held there until the day of judgment. It has been said that both verses refer to the enigmatic passage in Genesis 6:1–4, that describes beings called *Nephilim* having sexual intercourse with women, intercourse the produced unusual offspring. Genesis 6:1–4 reads:

When men began to multiply on the face of the ground, and

daughters were born of them, the sons of God saw that the daughters of men were fair; and they took to wife such of them as they chose. Then the LORD said, "My spirit shall not abide in man forever, for he is flesh, but his days shall be a hundred and twenty years." The Nephilim were on the earth in those days, and also afterward, when the sons of God came in to the daughters of men, and they bore children to them. These were the mighty men that were of old, the men of renown.

The *Nephilim* or the mysterious "sons of God" have been viewed as angels who sinned by having sexual intercourse with women. Because of the sinful act, the *Nephilim* (assumed to be angels) or "sons of God" (beings which may or may not be the same as the *Nephilim*) are cast out of heaven (their proper dwelling place). However one might wish to interpret Genesis 6:1–4, to link this passage with the verses in 2 Peter and Jude seems to pose far more problems than it would solve. But 2 Peter 2:4 and Jude 6 clearly assert that the rebellious angels are being kept prisoner int the "nether gloom." If they are prisoners, they could not very well function as the demons are described as functioning in the New Testament. These two passages, however, allow one to make a solid guess that the demons are indeed fallen angels.

In Matthew 25:41 Jesus refers to angels belonging to Satan. Again, it may be said that a good guess, based on this statement, is the demons are fallen angels.

The Bible, then, does not specifically present an account of the origin of demons, even if Isaiah 14:12–20 and Ezekiel 28:11–19 are used as explanations of the origin of Satan. Unger has reached the same conclusion. He says, "Concerning the precise origin of the demons though, nothing dogmatic ought to be asserted or insisted upon, inasmuch as this is one phase of the subject affected by the problem of the silence of revelation."[31]

THE NATURE OF DEMONS

The subject of the nature of demons presents fewer difficulties than their origin. It is conclusive that the Bible presents one devil and many demons. The number of demons is uncertain since the Bible makes no

---

[31] Ibid.

reference to that point; yet it seems their number is very large. Satan, though, is the ruler and director of the unclean spirits. Foerster is very clear about the relationship between Satan and demons when he says, "In the New Testament demons are completely subject to Satan."[32]

Jesus and the relationship between Satan and demons. Jesus speaks of "the devil and his angels" in Matthew 25:41. Although the angels mentioned are not called demons we deduce that they are. The link between Satan and demons is more easily demonstrated in the Pharisees' accusation of Jesus that He was possessed by Beelzebul, prince of demons."[33] The passage in question is Matthew 12:22–29:

> *Then a blind and dumb demoniac was brought to him, and he healed him, so that the dumb man spoke and saw. And all the people were amazed, and said, "Can this be the Son of David?" But when the Pharisees heard it they said, "It is only by Beelzebul, the prince of demons, that this man casts out demons." Knowing their thoughts, he said to them, "Every kingdom divided against itself is laid waste, and no city or house divided against itself will stand: and if Satan casts out Satan, he is divided against himself; how then will his kingdom stand? And if I cast out demons by Beelzebul, by whom do your sons cast them out? Therefore they shall be your judges. But if it is by the Spirit of God that I cast out demons, then the kingdom of God has come upon you. Or how can one enter a strong man's house and plunder his goods, unless he first binds the strong man? Then indeed he may plunder his house.*

After seeing Jesus cast demons out of a blind and dumb demoniac evidenced by a healing, the Pharisees accused Jesus of casting out demons by Beelzebul, prince of demons. Jesus reacted to the

---

[32] Foerster, op. cit., p. 18.

[33] Matthew 12:22–29; Mark 3:22–27; and Luke 11:14–22. For further references to Beelzebul, Belial, Samuel, and other names associated with Satan see: Edward Langton, *Essentials of Demonology* (London: The Epworth Press, 1949), chap. 6; *The Interpreter's Dictionary of the Bible* (New York: Abingdon Press, 1962), under the appropriate headings; and Gerhard Kittel, *Theological Dictionary of the New Testament* (Grand Rapids: Wm. B. Eerdmans Publishing Co., 1964), vol. 2, pp. 1–20.

accusation by saying, in Matthew 12:26, "And if Satan cast out Satan, he is divided against himself; how then will his kingdom stand?" Jesus' reply indicated that He assumed the reference to be concerned with Satan. Thus, the parallel is made between Satan and demons; they are related in that demons being cast out of a man is the same as Satan being cast out of a man.

John 8:39–47 is a passage that helps us understand the nature of Satan. The relevant verse is John 8:44. It reads:

> You are of your father the devil, and your will is to do your father's desires. He was a murderer from the beginning, and has nothing to do with the truth, because there is no truth in him. When he lies, he speaks according to his own nature, for he is a liar and the father of lies.

Jesus was speaking to Jews and not to demons, but Satan's character is discussed in the verse. The nature of demons is like that of their ruler, Satan. Satan is revealed as a murderer and a liar, actually the first and chief murderer and liar. Demons devotedly follow in the footsteps of the devil. As murderers, demons oppose God's creation; as liars, they are concerned with deceiving men and distorting the truth of God.

Summary statement. Satan and his demons are opposed to God and thus are committed only to themselves and to evil. The nature of demons as well as Satan is autonomous self-centeredness. It is their nature to be against God. Satan did not create the demons, but he is over them in authority. It is also clear that where the demons are, there also is Satan. The demons are evil as Satan is evil; there is no such thing as a "good" demon. The purpose of demons is the purpose of Satan; they are in total opposition to God and are thereby opposed to God's creation.

Demons are spiritual beings[34] in that they do not have flesh and blood bodies, require nothing material for life or sustenance, are generally not visible,[35] and can have personal influence with people

---

[34] Biblical passages on demons having spiritual bodies are Matthew 8:16; 17:18; Mark 9:25; Luke 10:17; Ephesians 2:2; 6:12.

[35] The following are passages which may point to the possibility of Satan and, correspondingly, demons being able to be seen: Genesis 3:1; Zechariah 3:1;

(especially in terms of indwelling people). Satan and demons are not spiritual in the sense that the angels of God are spiritual or in the sense that the Trinity is spiritual. Satan and his demons are spiritual powers of evil and darkness that are opposed to God.

Demons have a personal quality to them. Unger says, "But it must not be supposed that because spirits are immaterial, they are any less personal.[36] They are personal in that they have intellect and knowledge and can influence the lives of men. In the New Testament, demons speak, they argue with Jesus, and in one instance they ask a favor of Him. However, they always obey Jesus' orders.[37] They are not personal as God is personal, nor are they personal as man is personal; yet, in a very qualified way, they have some characteristics that are personal in nature. Heinrich Schlier describes there personality in the following manner:

> The New Testament teaches on the one hand that the demonical powers are a kind of personal beings. ...but what is meant by "personal beings"? It means that they manifest themselves as beings of intellect and will, which can speak and be spoken to. They are something which is capable of purposeful activity.[38]

Satan may not properly be referred to as "he," and demons may certainly not be called persons in the sense that a man is a person. Yet the Greek New Testament uses personal pronouns for both Satan and demons.[39]

It may be concluded that the Bible does not explicitly describe in

---

Matthew 4:9, 10; 2 Corinthians 11:14. The occult furnishes a great deal of evidence for the materialization of demons. For examples of photographs of supposed demons manifestations see: Katherine Beaton-Troker, *Psychic Experiences* (New York: Vantage Press, 1962), and Edward L. Gardner, *Fairies* (London: The Theosophical Publishing House, London, 1966).

[36] Unger, op. cit., p. 64.

[37] See references: Matthew 8:28–34; Mark1:23–26; 3:11–12; 5:1–13; Luke 4:33–37: 8:26–39.

[38] Heinrich Schlier , *Principalities and Powers in the New Testament* (New York: Herder and Herder, 1961), p. 18.

[39] See references: Matthew 4:7; 8:29; Mark 1:24; 5:7; Luke 4:34; 8:28.

full the nature of demons, but it describes them well enough for them to be distinguished amidst the hosts of God's creation.

DISCUSSION QUESTIONS

1. Explain how the warnings against demonic practices in the Old Testament (i.e., Deuteronomy 18:9–13) suggest pagan influences.

2. Explain and illustrate the three principles of Old Testament demonology.

3. What might some of Jesus' Galilean friends have believed about spirits and demons? What kind of demonology might a first century Roman emperor have had?

4. Is all desire for knowledge demonic? If not, what kind of a desire for knowledge is demonic?

5. Why do you think the term *exorkizo* and *horkizo* are not used to describe a Christian casting out demons? How does this illustrate the principle of power?

6. Outline the central aspect of Jesus' ministry to the demonized.

7. How does Satan's temptation of Jesus illustrate two principles of demonology? How do these principles differ from the principles of power and knowledge?

8. Is it necessary to understand precisely the origin of Satan and demons? Why or why not?

9. How are Satan and demons related?

10. Demons have "personal" qualities. How does their "personality" differ from that of men or angels?

Christianity, the only true religion, has alone demonstrated that the gods of the nations are most impure demons, who desire to be thought gods, availing themselves of the names of certain dead souls, or the appearance of mundane creatures, and with proud impurity rejoicing in things most base and infamous, as though in divine honors, and envying human souls their conversion to the true God.

ST. AUGUSTINE
The City of God

4
Principles of Demonology

Four principles of demonology have emerged from the biblical material. They are (1) the desire for knowledge; (2) the desire for power; (3) the frustration, distortion, or perversion of the will of God; and (4) the worship of Satan. These are not meant to be rigid classifications, but they are convenient tools for understanding contemporary demonology.

In addition, there are six principles of non-biblical demonology: (1) a desire to experience the supernatural; (2) a desire to be religious apart from Christian commitment and repentance; (3) a rationale and environment for immoral activity; (4) a rebellion against organized Christianity; (5) a desire for assurance of a life beyond the grave; and (6) the demonic as a counterfeit. These principles have grown out of the writer's experience and observation of the contemporary occult because the Scriptures do not provide an adequate basis for classifying these as strictly biblical principles of demonology.

In this chapter the biblical and extra-biblical principles of demonology will be discussed with a view toward applying them to the contemporary occult practices in chapter 5.

PRINCIPLES OF BIBLICAL DEMONOLOGY

KNOWLEDGE AND POWER

Due to close connections between the principles of the desire for knowledge and the desire for power, they will be considered under the same major heading. Much that can be said of one can be said of the other. Some distinctions between two principles may seem arbitrary.

Joseph Bayly, writing on the common element of witchcraft, points out that those engaged in witchcraft want something beyond their grasp.[1] What is desired may be summarized in terms of seeking after knowledge or power. Such seeking necessitates an intermediary, demons, spirits, or other forces which are manipulated through the vehicle of witchcraft (magic).

Merrill Unger likewise links the principles of knowledge and power with the occult. He writes, "The desire and drive for knowledge and power in opposition to the command will of God constitutes the essence of magic."[2]

Kurt Koch has observed the principles of knowledge and power in the occult. He speaks of the urge that drives people into the occult as being a will to power, a desire to know what God knows.[3] Speaking of magic in particular, Koch says, "Magic is the very antithesis of the commandment of God as it reveals a hunger for knowledge and a desire for power in opposition to the will of God."[4]

Knowledge. To seek knowledge is, in a sense, to seek power, so this section on knowledge will be brief. The major thrust will be on the principle of power.

Divination, a special type of magic, refers to fortune-telling. Divination may involve such practices as astrology, augury, card reading, psychic reading, crystal gazing, necromancy, numerology, palmistry, and soothsaying. The desire to know the events of tomorrow leads directly to the occult. A *Time* magazine article on the demonic said,

---

[1] Joseph Bayly, *What about Horoscopes?* (Elgin, Ill.: David C. Cook Publishing Co., 1970), p. 26.

[2] Merrill F. Unger, *Demons in the World Today* (Wheaton, Ill.: Tyndale House Publishing, 1971), p. 80

[3] Kurt Koch, *Christian Counseling and Occultism* (Grand Rapid: Kregel Publications, 1965), p. 6

[4] Kurt Koch, *Between Christ and Satan* (Baden: Evangelization Publishers, 1967), pp. 61–62. In this same book, Koch writes of the double nature of magic as understood by parapsychology (the study of extrasensory perception). Parapsychology distinguishes between Psi-gamma phenomena and Psi-kappa phenomena. "Psi" stands for para-psychical phenomena, while "gamma" represents the Greek word, *gignoskein*, "to perceive, " and "kappa" represents the Greek word, *kinein*, "to move." In this distinction are seen the two basic elements of magic: knowledge and power.

"One anxiety the occultists share with the rest of mankind is about the future. They want to know it, and many of them believe that they can glimpse it."[5] For example, Goethe's Faust strove for an all-encompassing knowledge, and in order to realize such knowledge, he made a pact with the devil. A person involves himself in astrology, palmistry, crystal gazing, and other forms of divination out of a desire to know the future, but in so doing exposes himself to the demonic. Men are tempted toward fortune-telling through a fear of the future or through a desire for control over people and events. The Bible, as already noted, discourages fortune-telling. Unger writes, "To seek intimate knowledge of the future is to impugn God's holy character."[6]

Satan has lots of knowledge. He has the second greatest computer and data analyzers in the universe. He has had all the data available to collect and evaluate. It is not a great chore for Satan to learn how to predict the future with considerable accuracy, so the occultist predictions of the future are no great thing. But it is often enough to convince and deceive the unsuspecting.

God is the great and wholly accurate source of knowledge. His predictions are recorded in the Bible; we call them prophecies, and they always come to pass. In contrast to Satan's deceptive prophesies God speaks of the future so that His people may prepare themselves for eternity.6

Power. Magic or witchcraft (the two terms have very similar meanings and are often used interchangeably) deals specifically with power. The second edition of Webster's New International Dictionary gives the following definitions of "magic":

> The art, or body of arts, which claims or is believed to be able to compel a deity or supernatural power to do or refrain from doing some act or to change temporarily the order of natural events, or which claims or is believed to produce effects by the assistance of supernatural beings, as angels, demons, or departed spirits, or by a mastery of secret forces in nature.

Susy Smith, a witch watcher, reports that "the ceremonies of

---

[5] "The Occult: A Substitute Faith," *Time*, 19 June 1972, p. 67.

[6] Unger, op. cit., p. 55.

witchcraft are elaborate rituals for summoning gods and goddesses—or devils and demons—to do one's bidding."[7] Donald Nugent states, "There seems to be certain common denominators found rather universally in witchcraft. It particularly orients around two things: sexuality... and power, often fusing the two."[8] And Anton La Vey, head of San Francisco's Satanic Church, wrote in his Satanic Bible, "No one ever pursued occult studies...without ego gratification and personal power as a goal."[9] A Time article said, "Power, and occultists and their critics agree, is at the core of the occult quest for self-realization.[10]

This principle was made very clear to me one day. A twenty-eight-year-old junior college student came to see me, for he had heard that I knew something about demon possession. He had worshiped Satan with Anton La Vey's group in San Francisco and became a member of the Church of Satan, having sold his soul to the devil. In exchange for his soul, he was to receive power to make money. It worked—he made lots of money with very little effort. Then he made a switch. Instead of power to make money, he wanted power over women. He received that, too. When he met woman he wanted, he would concentrate on her. Before the day was out, the woman would either show up at his door or call him on the phone. He came to me because the woman told him that he was strange. Several told him he was demonic. After we'd talked a long while, he reached a conclusion: he didn't want Jesus because, he said, "I'd lose my power."

What emerges, then, in regard to the occult or the demonic, is that power—a seeking or desire for power—is an important principle of demonology. Many occult practices seek to manipulate spiritual power: the occultist wants to command the transcendent authority. The occultist wants to have "God" at his disposal. Such arrogance is actually at the heart of the occult, which makes it rather simple for the Christian to grasp its significance. In the two basic categories of magic—black and white—the essence of the practices is evident. The

---

[7] Susy Smith, *Today's Witches* (Englewood Cliffs, N. J.: Prentice Hall, Inc., 1970), p. 3.

[8] Donald Nugent, "The Renaissance and Rise of Witchcraft," *Church History*, 40 (March 1971): 71.

[9] Anton La Vey, *The Satanic Bible* (New York: Avon 1969), p. 110.

[10] "The Occult: A Substitute Faith," loc. cit.

enchantments of black magic are for the purposes of persecution, vengeance, defense, or healing. The enchantments of white magic are for the purposes of protection, defense, healing or fruitfulness. The enchantments are essentially procedures whereby gods, demons, angels, or other powers are manipulated to produce the desired end.

IMPEDING THE WILL OF GOD

Demons oppose God and aim to impede His will. The demonic corrupts everything that comes under the influence of its fascinating attractiveness. Wilbur M. Smith, in his introduction to Unger's Biblical Demonology, says the constant mission of supernatural beings or demons is "to deceive, and degrade, and destroy men."[11]

The purpose of the demonic is to pervert, distort, or frustrate the will of God. In terms of Christian thought this is a generalization, almost a truism that can have wide application. Yet, this third principle finds a clear application in regard to the demonic. It is clear from the Bible that God desires man to be healthy and whole. God seeks to save man. The demonic, on the other hand, is concerned to demonize man, and whatever may be said of demonization, it is clear that it does disrupt the normal life of the possessed. Werner Foerster, writing on the view of demons in the New Testament, says, "In most stories of possession what is at issue is not merely sickness but a destruction and distortion of the divine likeness of man according to creation."[12] He also says in regard to the New Testament view of demons:

> Yet it confirms the popular sense of something horrible and sinister in such spirits, bringing out the demonic nature of their activity as an attack on the spiritual and physical life of man in fulfillment of the will of Satan.[13]

Satan's will is directly opposed to God's will. And through the demonic, particularly the occult with or without demonization, Satan

---

[11] Merrill F. Unger, *Biblical Demonology* (Wheaton, Ill.: Scripture Press, 1952), p. xiii.

[12] Werner Foerster in *Theological Dictionary of the New Testament,* ed. Gerhard Kettle and trans. Geoffrey W. Bromiley (Grand Rapids: Wm. B. Eerdmans Publishing Co., 1964), vol. 2, pp. 18–19.

[13] Ibid, p. 19.

is able to execute his will. Victor Ernest, a Baptist minister who in his early adulthood, before his conversion to Christ, had been a spiritualist medium, says:

> Their unholy mission is to lead human beings—by refined or gross means—away from dependence on God, their Creator, and they are active in spiritualist churches, séances, psychic phenomena, witchcraft, and idol-worship.[14]

This third principle of opposition to God's will may be too broad to apply adequately to many instances of contemporary occultism. Yet, setting the third principle apart aids in analyzing some occult practices.

SATAN WORSHIP

There is a sense in which all demonic practices can be called Satan worship. Contact with demons is similar to or the same as contact with Satan; where demons are, Satan is also. The purpose of Satan is the purpose of his demons.

Occult practices encourage and often demand openness to spirits. Spirits are invoked or conjured by some occult practitioners for various purposes. Some forms of the occult demand a passive state of mind on the part of the participants so that the "spirits" might be contacted. The occult medium is purposely trained to enter into passive or altered states of mind so that a trance state (an openness to "spirits"), might be achieved. This activity is essentially Satan worship.

Demonic services like those of Anton La Vey's Satanic Church are clear examples of direct and purposeful worship of Satan. Ernest says, "Satan is openly honored, of course, by some practitioners of the so-called 'black arts' or 'black magic.'"[15] However, in the occult, open and expressed Satan worship is the exception rather than the rule. Most occultists believe they are in contact with good or neutral spirits, not suspecting that these spirits are demons. Much Satan worship in the occult, then is in disguise. Instead of placating or using good spirits or spirit guides, occultists are actually trafficking with demons.

---

[14] Victor Ernest, *I Talked With Spirits* (Wheaton, Ill.: Tyndale House Publishers, 1970), p. 18.

[15] Ibid, p.44.

A group of young people I met on the street responded to my witness by saying that they were religious and actually had angels helping them to worship. I was not too impressed with that because so many white magicians I knew had "angels" as helpers or guides.

They told me how an "angel" first came to them. They had been fasting and meditating, and they were consciously waiting for visions. Visions did come, but so did a being they thought was an angel. It appeared white and transparent, not fully formed but very real. It gave them a powerful sense of the supernatural, but there was also something eerie about it. The angel constantly reassured them about their worship, and encouraged them to be moral and stop using drugs. They were elated and were proud of their new faith. Jesus and the Bible were left out for the most part, but they were more tolerant of Jesus than many nonbelievers. However, it was not Christ but the "angel" who had taken first place in their lives. They followed his instructions, believed his teaching, and obeyed his commands. To bring the angel into their presence, all they needed to do was form a circle, join hands, and concentrate. Their angel was an "angel of light," like that one Paul referred to when he wrote, "And no wonder, for even Satan disguises himself as an angel of light. So it is not strange if his servants also disguise themselves as servants of righteousness."[16]

Demons accept religious worship and desire communion with men. The demonic even propagates its own doctrine. To worship Satan, to believe his doctrine, is—from a Biblical viewpoint—against the will of God. Viewing Satan worship in this manner, we see that its relation to the principle of the perversion of the will of God is very close. Yet, making the distinction between the two principles will help in examining contemporary occult practices.

PRINCIPLES OF NON-BIBLICAL DEMONOLOGY

A DESIRE TO EXPERIENCE THE SUPERNATURAL

Modern technological societies have left little room for the transcendent aspect of human existence. The occult is mysterious and spiritual—it fascinates. To most people, the occult seems to promise a new religious experience—a new religious world full of spirits, rituals,

---

[16] 2 Corinthians 11:14, 15

and exotic experiences. Parapsychology, having come to the aid of the occult, has adequately demonstrated to many people's satisfaction a spiritual reality above and beyond the normal physical existence. There is a certain fascination in the occult, and for some the fascination becomes something akin to a compulsion to experience whatever it is that makes the demonic work. And these practices do work. Tables move and make knocking sounds, apparitions of the deceased are seen, telepathy produces results, mediumistic predictions come true, psychic readings prove to be incredibly accurate, and conversations with the "departed" are regular occurrences in séances. The occult *is* supernatural.

Some occult practitioners have sincerely attached themselves to the "religion," others have lightly and frivolously exposed themselves to the occult; but for many, their initial involvement grew out of a desire to experience the supernatural.

The occult is a religious practice. It requires a real commitment of one's life. Such a commitment may mean partaking in rituals, repeating oaths or incantations, and assuming a passive state of mind to allow spiritual forces freedom in a group meeting or direct access to the mind (i.e., the séance). An occult practice may have religious trappings as well. In many spiritualist churches, hymns are sung, prayers are said, the Bible is read, readings or prophecy given (usually in mediumistic fashion through trance), and people are urged to be moral and religious. In white magic, the name of Jesus may even be used in incantations or prayers. Trinity formulas commonly appear in magical rituals and incantations. Fortune-tellers particularly like to claim that God is the source of their knowledge. Jeane Dixon is one fortune-teller who claims to base her entire work on God and the Bible; Edgar Cayce, the late clairvoyant and predictor, was biblically oriented in some ways. Occultists seem to out-religionize, out-moralize, and out-supernaturalize some variations of Christianity. The occult is thoroughly and convincingly supernatural, and because it is, it draws people. It often attracts nominal Christians who feel alienated and lonely. Such groups may combine a personal and sacred dimension. The mysterious evil overtones and in-group type of setting, under which occult activities often operate, provide an additional lure.

A Desire to be Religious Apart from Christian Commitment and Repentance

The occultist often refers to himself as a religious person. Satanists, for example, consider themselves as committed religionists with a satanology to match the Christian's theology. But it is a religion that avoids repentance and commitment to Jesus Christ. Sandy Simmons, writing in *Home Missions*, a Southern Baptist publication, says, "There is no sin in the eyes of the Church of Satan."[17]

Commitment to Christ and repentance are two aspects of one's Christian experience, and both are carefully avoided by the occultist. An occultist may identify himself as a Christian, may attend church, and strive to be a good, moral citizen. Joseph Bayly quotes Sybil Leek, a modern-day witch, as saying that people are searching for "a religion where they don't have to live a Godlike life."[18] The occult is a religion that usually asks for a moral life, but does not demand turning from sin to Christ. The claims of Jesus are particularly detested by most occultists. They prefer to see Him as a great prophet, the elder brother, a great medium, a great teacher, a great psychic, or even a powerful magician or sorcerer. They reject Christ's claim to be the only Savior and mediator between God and man. The Jesus of most occultists is anything but the Jesus of the Bible.

A psychic healer regularly spoke of Jesus in her group sessions. One night several friends and I passed out Christian literature to those arriving for her weekly session. The medium was irritated by our presence and heatedly asked us to leave. The psychic readings were held, by the way, in a church building. The pastor of the church thought it was all quite Christian. I asked the psychic one direct question about Jesus being the God-man; she said she adored Jesus and looked to Him as the Great Psychic Healer. I then asked if she had any biblical support for her position; she said she didn't need any.

A Rationale and Environment for Immoral Activities

The occult establishment has sometimes provided a cloak for sexual

---

[17] Sandy Simmons, "The Devil Made Me Do It," *Home Missions*, January 1972, p. 42.

[18] Bayly, op. cit., p. 27.

excess and drug abuse. At the same time, the occult has openly practiced forms of immorality. The sabbat (witches sabbat) is notorious for its sexual orgies. As previously quoted, Donald Nugent states that one of the common denominators of witchcraft is sexuality (as symbol or as fact).[19] Victor Ernest, in speaking of some practitioners of black magic, says, "These people are obsessed with hexes and spells, sexual indulgences, weird rituals, and hints of violence."[20] My counseling experience has shown that immorality is more common in youth subcultural groups involved in the occult than in the middle class occult establishments.

A group engaged in occult activities often finds that the occult orientation easily lends itself to sexual immorality and to the use of drugs or alcohol. The rational provided, the practical aspects of the occult activity are free to move toward immorality and the misuse of drugs. A friend of mine, a new convert, said the group he joined to study witchcraft turned out to be a group of swingers and wife-swappers. They weren't even serious occultists. Even the owner of an occult book store in our county is constantly involved with drugs and group sex. Another occult group that meets in our county regularly practices perverted forms of group sex in conjunction with black magic.

A REBELLION AGAINST ORGANIZED CHRISTIANITY

People in the hip-youth counterculture have found participation in the occult a good way of getting back at Christian parents or of striking out at "Christian" America. The occult has been anti-establishment, and it therefore satisfies the rebellious orientation of many people. In the past, the occult was patronized mostly by the poor or working class peoples as commitment would demand that they turn away from and confess this rebellion, while the occult may even foster such an attitude. The church, or society in general, often seems to be a source of repression and censorship, but the occult is nonthreatening to persons desiring sinful expression. The occult appears enough like a religion, especially when it is promoted through mass media, to provide an alternative to a person who is reacting against Christianity.

---

[19] Nugent, loc. cit.

[20] Ernest, op. cit., p. 44. Also see: "The Occult: A Substitute Faith," loc. cit., p. 66.

A *Time* article reports, "Time and again, converts from traditional religions relate how they resented being told what to do by their priests or ministers, how the occult give them freedom to do what they want, seek what they want."[21] There is quite a difference between obedience to Jesus and obedience to the devil. No repentance is needed to become one of Satan's disciples. A fifteen-year-old Satan worshiper I knew in Haight-Ashbury said he went into it to avoid Christianity. Another girl told me that her astrology and palm reading didn't interfere with her sexual promiscuity. Nearly every occultist I've met has been antagonistic to Jesus and the Bible.

A DESIRE FOR ASSURANCE OF LIFE BEYOND THE GRAVE

Out of what seemed like remorse, even guilt, the late Bishop James Pike sought through spiritualist séances to establish communication with his son Jim, who had committed suicide. Bishop Pike's visit to a spiritualist medium in hopes of contacting the dead is often repeated by people who either want assurance of an afterlife or want to communicate with a deceased loved one. Since the occult is real and does work, many people have been deceived into thinking that they actually contacted the "other side." Christianity teaches that the deceased are beyond human reach and prohibits attempting to contact them (Deut. 18:10, 11). Yet the occult, particularly spiritualism, clearly teaches that the "other side" is accessible.

Before I knew much about the occult, I made a rather serious mistake in counseling a woman whose husband had recently died. She wanted to contact him to see if he was in heaven or hell. He had not been a Christian, and she felt guilty because of her poor witness. When she expressed the desire to visit a medium, I simply *let it go*—I didn't know what a medium was. Her problem was that she could not locate one. However, one day she received a letter in the mail from a medium who offered her assistance. Thankfully, by this time the woman had passed through her grief, and her faith was growing. She did not consult the medium.

---

[21] "The Occult: A Substitute Faith," loc. cit.

THE DEMONIC AS A COUNTERFEIT

The demonic is spiritual. God, too, is a Spirit, but spiritual as nothing else can be. The spirituality of the occult, while not fully understood, is non-spiritual or anti-spiritual, but still spiritual. The occult is spiritual enough to counterfeit the truly spiritual. Contact with the spirituality of the occult has led people to commit themselves to it. People have felt that because the occult is spiritual it must be from God. In some occult practices, authentic spiritual gifts are counterfeited. Occultists often identify their visions and predictions as prophesy. They often teach that astrological predictions and predictions based on palm readings are prophecy from God.[22] Occultists may simulate the authentic spiritual gifts of speaking in tongues and the interpretation of tongues.[23]

Counterfeits of the demonic are clever and not easily spotted by the inexperienced. The spiritual gift of discernment, as recorded in 1 Corinthians 12:10, has an application at this point. The Holy Spirit, according to Jesus, convicts people of sin, judgment, and righteousness,[24] whereas the power behind the occult excuses sin, denies judgment, and promotes self-attained morality. The Holy Spirit also testifies of, points to, honors, and glorifies Jesus Christ.[25]

The gifts of God's Spirit produce good fruit and glorify the Savior, Jesus Christ. There are real spiritual gifts in operation today. Many of the spiritual gifts I've seen in charismatic spiritual circles are genuine. It is in the spiritualist groups that the spiritual gifts are most often counterfeited. Being acquainted with both the charismatic and counterfeit spiritual gifts, the distinctions are quite clear to me. There is no fear, no confusion, no blasphemy of Jesus or the Bible when the Holy Spirit is moving. Neither are there people in what seem to

---

[22] 1 Corinthians 12:4–10 lists nine spiritual gifts, gifts that may occur or be manifested during an assembly of believers, and are often counterfeited by the demonic. Romans 12:6–8 also contains a list of spiritual gifts.

[23] Raphael Gasson, in his book, *The Challenging Counterfeit* (Plainfield, N. J.: Logos International, 1966), explains how occultists, particularly spiritualists, copy or counterfeit biblical spiritual gifts. Chapters 7–12 especially deal with such counterfeits.

[24] John 16:8–11

[25] John 15:26 and 16:14–15

be trance-like states. The Holy Spirit does not drain the believer of strength, but the occult worshiper is often tired to the point of exhaustion. The Spirit-filled believer praises and rejoices in Jesus Christ. The occultist does not.

DISCUSSION QUESTIONS

1. Astrology is practiced by many people, yet it illustrates the principle of knowledge. How is astrology similar to crystal ball gazing and psychic readings of mediums?

2. Some forms of "Christian" worship closely resemble white magic practices. How might a Christian become "power" oriented, and how might this be expressed?

3. Occultists usually don't see themselves as opposed to God. How might a Christian explain the principle of the frustration of the will of God to an occultist?

4. How is it that an astrologer or a clairvoyant is a Satan worshiper?

5. How could a person who is hungering for a supernatural experience or religion be satisfied with the occult?

6. What is the place of repentance and faith in the occult? How can Christianity be altered to accommodate occult practices?

7. Many occult practices are neither gross nor immoral. What connections are there between sexual immorality and the occult?

8. How is the practice of ESP a rebellion against Christianity?

9. How might Satan and his demons convince a person of the reality of life after death and at the same time steer a person away from the truth of Jesus and the resurrection?

10. What are some principles by which the pseudo-spirituality of the occult can be detected?

I was at this party, about eight months ago, where you were greeted at the door with a glass of special hallucinogenic formula: acids and a pinch of strychnine. Rat poison. Makes the trip very physical. You went in and there were three altars. On two of them, these boys were tied with leather thongs. They were sobbing. These two faggots dressed as nuns—one had a goatee—were beating them with big black rosaries. On the middle altar was a very young girl. This guy wearing a goat's head had crushed a live frog on her privates. When I came in, he had just cut a little cross on her stomach; not deep, but the party had just started.

AN ANONYMOUS GIRL
Esquire, March 1970

5
Contemporary Occultism
and
Demonic Possession

EXPLOSION OF THE OCCULT

During the past several years, the occult has ceased being confined to the underground and has moved into the open. Joseph Bayly says, "Salem was too much for the New World to stomach. Salem drove witchcraft underground for almost three centuries of 'Enlightenment.' Now it's been exhumed on a new winter's afternoon before the fire, as fun and games."[1]

Occult literature is no longer difficult to obtain but is readily accessible to most people. It is being beamed at what is not usually called "middle America," "the silent majority," or "consensus—U.S.A."

The occult is big business. As early as 1970, Sybil Leek, a professional witch, cited some impressive statistics.

> Of America's 1,750 newspapers, more than 1,200 now carry a regular astrology column, and most national magazines have their own astrologers. Twenty years ago, the total number of newspapers and magazines interested in astrology was scarcely more than a hundred. Today the astrology magazines, monthlies, and annuals have a prominent place on newsstands throughout the country.[2]

The occult trend has been steadily up since 1970, to the point that involvement with the occult has almost become an "in" or "acceptable"

---

[1] Joseph Bayly, *What About Horoscopes?* (Elgin, Ill.: David C. Cook Publishing Co., 1970), p. 38

[2] Sybil Leek, *Astrology Journal*, April 1970, p. 221.

hobby or religion. This is one of the few instances, if not the only one, in history when the occult has enjoyed such broad popular support. Usually it is underground and rejected by the majority. Paul prophesied that in the last days there would be an outbreak of the demonic. He said that in the last times there would be people giving heed to "deceitful spirits and doctrines of demons" (1 Tim. 4:1). The demonic is so deceitful that it succeeds in leading astray those who know better. The demonic in the last days not only is deceitful, that is, seeming to be other than what it really is (such as ESP), but it also comes with a set of evil doctrines. Yet, if the occult revival is just another fad, its consequences are rather more dramatic than the "hula hoop" craze.

PHASES OF THE OCCULT AND PRINCIPLES OF DEMONOLOGY

The occult has many faces. It is not an easy task to distinguish clearly between some of its forms. For example, a witch or sorcerer may be involved in magic, fortune-telling, and spiritism all at the same time. Necromancy illustrates the problem: it involves contacting what are thought to be deceased spirits (spiritism or spiritualism)[3] through some type of ritual or ceremony (magic), for the purpose of obtaining something, usually knowledge, from the spirit (fortune-telling). There is much overlapping in the various occult practices, but they may be divided into three broad categories for the purpose of study: magic, fortune-telling, and spiritism.

MAGIC

Types of magic. The three commonly designated types of magic are white, black, and neutral. Basically, white magic is said to involve itself with good spirits or gods for innocent purposes. Black magic is said to involve itself with bad spirits or gods for evil purposes. Practitioners

---

[3] Spiritism and spiritualism are essentially the same. Spiritism often lacks the religious touch of spiritualism. Both concentrate on the contacting of spirits, but spiritism is the older and cruder form. Spiritualism is intellectually and morally on a higher plane than spiritism. Spiritualism borrows some aspects of orthodox Christian worship such as prayer, Bible reading, hymn singing, preaching, and the use of Christian symbols. Spiritualism and spiritism will be combined here under the single heading of spiritism.

of white magic are referred to as white magicians or witches, and practitioners of black magic are referred to as black magicians or witches. Neutral magic is said to involve itself with neutral forces of nature. However, magic is magic, whether it is white, black, or neutral, since the principle of power is characteristic of all three forms.

The distinctions between the three types of magic are superficial. Some general areas of applied magic are the healing and causing of diseases, love-and-hate magic, charms, spells, curses, persecution-and-defense magic, and death magic. Extrasensory perception (telepathy, clairvoyance, etc.) and mediumistic hypnosis may be classed under neutral magic. These phenomena are difficult to classify and will not be discussed as such in this chapter, although much of what is said in terms of magic, fortune-telling , and spiritism does apply to para-psychological phenomena. Telepathy, clairvoyance, clairaudience, automatic writing, and similar phenomena often have to do with knowledge, but more especially with power. A certain high school girl used ESP at parties. She could say who was coming before there was a knock at the door, she could guess cards and tell fortunes. She gained quite a reputation. Others respected her for her knowledge and power. It was fun and games to most of her friends, but as for the girl herself, the desire for more knowledge and power gained a demonic hold on her.

Merrill Unger defines magic as "the art of bringing about results beyond man's power through the enlistment of supernatural agencies."[4] Magic involves the commanding or impelling of supernatural forces. The demonological principle of power is clearly seen in magic.

Magic enchantments. Henry Wedeck, in his *Treasury of Witchcraft*, gives example of magic enchantments. In an enchantment entitled "Summoning the Spirits," the demonological principle of power is plainly evident.

> I conjure thee, Spirit, by the Living God, by the true God, by the blessed and omnipotent God: He who created the Heavens, and Earth, the Sea, and all the things that are in them, from out of nothing.

---

[4] Merrill F. Unger, *Biblical Demonology* (Wheaton, Ill.: Scripture Press, 1952), p. 108.

In the Name of Jesus Christ, by the power of the Holy Sacraments and of the Eucharist, and in the power of this Son of God who was crucified, who died, and who was buried, for our sake. He who rose again, on the Third Day, and who is now seated at the right of the Supreme Creator, and from where He will come to be a judge over the living and over the dead; and likewise by the priceless love of the Holy Spirit, and Perfect Trinity.

I conjure thee into this circle, O accursed spirit, thou, who has dared to disobey God. I exercise thee, Serpent, and I order thee to appear immediately, in human form, well-shaped, in body and soul, and so comply with my commands without deception of whatsoever kind, and without either mental reservation: and this by the Great Names of God, the God of Gods and the Lord of all Lords:

Adonay, Tetragrammaton, Jehova, Tetragrammaton, Adonay, Jehova, Otheos, Athanatos, Ischyros, Agla, Pentagrammaton, Saday, Saday, Saday, Jehova, Otheos, Athanotos, Aliciat Tetragrammaton, Adonay, Ischyros, Athanatos, Sady, Sady, Sady Cados, Cados, Cados, Eloy, Agla, Agla, Agla, Adonay, Adonay:

I conjure thee, O evil and accursed Serpent, to appear at my wish and pleasure, in this place and before this Circle, immediately, alone and without any companion, without any ill-will, delay, noise, deformity or evasion. I also exorcise thee by the ineffable names of God, namely, Gog and Magog, which I am not worthy to speak. Come here, come here, come here. Satisfy me and my commands, without evasion or lie. If thou does not this, Saint Michael, the invisible Archangel will soon stick thee in the deepest of Hell.

Come then, and obey me, and accomplish my desire.[5]

Wedeck clearly points out the purpose of magic. He says:

---

[5] Henry Wedeck, *Treasury of Witchcraft* (New York: Philosophical Library, 1961), p. 185.

The magical incantation was an occult formula, known only to the ancient priest-magicians, or to the witch-doctor, or to the practicing adept, whose purpose was to summon an infernal power, to bewitch an enemy, to produce a phenomenon not arising from normal causes. [6]

Conjuring spirits or even conjuring Satan himself is characteristic of magic. Occasionally the names of the Trinity are used in conjurations. This is particularly so in white magic. The names of the Trinity are used in magical practices so that the divine powers will come under the influence or to the aid of the magician. The purpose of using divine names in magic is to accomplish the obedience of all spirits of forces over which the names are pronounced. Arthur Waite, an expert on magic, describes it as a search for God, but it is clear that magic is an attempt to use God or the supernatural to accomplish the will of the magician. Waite gives the following example of a ritual of transcendental magic. It demonstrates the use of the names of the Trinity and other orthodox Christian expressions and symbols.

Enlighten mine eyes with true light, that they may never be closed in eternal sleep, lest mine enemy should say: I have prevailed over him. So long as the Lord is with me, I will not fear for malice of my enemies. O most sweet Jesus, preserve me, aid me, save me; at the Name of Jesus let every knee bow, in heaven, on earth and in Hell, and let every tongue confess openly that Jesus Christ is in the glory of His Father, Amen. I know beyond doubt that in what day soever I shall call upon the Lord, in the same hour shall I be saved. O most sweet Lord Jesus Christ, Son of the great living God, Thou has performed most mighty miracles by the sole power of Thy most precious Name, and has enriched the poor most abundantly, so that by force thereof the demons flee away, the blind see, the deaf hear, the lame walk erect, the dumb speak, the lepers are cleansed, the sick cured, the dead raised up; for wheresoever the most sweet Name of Jesus is pronounced, the ear is ravished and the mouth is filled with pleasant savor; at that one utterance, I repeat, the demons take flight, every knee is bent,

---

[6] Ibid, p.15.

all temptations, even the worst, are scattered, all infirmities are healed, all disputes and conflicts between the world, the flesh and the Devil are ended, and the soul is filled with every heavenly delight; for whosoever invoketh or shall invoke this Holy Name of God is and shall be saved—even by this Holy Name, pronounced by the angel even before His conception in the womb of the Holy Virgin.[7]

I was amazed to discover the use of the name of Jesus and other Christian expressions in magic enchantments. It confuses me because of what the Apostle John said about the testing of spirits.

Beloved, do not believe every spirit, but test the spirits to see whether they are of God: for many false prophets have gone out into the world. By this you know the Spirit of God: every spirit which confesses that Jesus Christ has come in the flesh is of God, and every spirit, which does not confess Jesus is not of God. This is the spirit of antichrist, of which you heard that it was coming, and now it is in the world already. (1 John 4:1–3)

The problem concerns what it means to confess that Jesus has come in the flesh. We know that it means that the Word of God, Jesus Himself, became flesh: Jesus is God, the God-man. But we know that simply to say, "Jesus has come in the flesh," is not necessarily an expression of Christian faith. Several times I have heard demons say, "Jesus has come in the flesh." The truth is that Satan and his demons are liars. Jesus referred to Satan as the father of lies (John 8:44), so it is nothing for a demon to lie about Jesus' coming in the flesh.

The same holds true for the confession, "Jesus is Lord." Paul said, "No one can say 'Jesus is Lord' except by the Holy Spirit." (1 Cor. 12:3b). To confess "Jesus is Lord" means that Jesus is your Lord, that is, Jesus has saved you and is now the Lord and master of your life. Demons can lie about it. In one of my first contacts with a demon-possessed person, I encountered a demon that repeatedly told me it was an "angel of light" and would say, "Jesus is Lord." The demon lied. Jesus Himself said, "On that day many will say to me, 'Lord, Lord, did we not

---

[7] Arthur Waite, *Book of Ceremonial Magic* (New York: University Books, 1961), p. 51.

prophesy in your name, and cast out demons in your name, and do many mighty works in your name?' and then will I declare to them, 'I never knew you; depart from me, you evildoers'" (Matthew 7:22, 23).

Waite described some of the powers granted through magic. Among them are (1) the ability to conjure spirits; (2) the love and compliance of men or women; (3) discovery of all treasures and ensuring their possession; (4) recovery of stolen goods; (5) the power to go invisible; (6) the winning of all games; (7) knowledge; and (8) the power to cause harm or death to animals or men.[8]

Magic principles. Magic illustrates two principles of demonology: power and a perversion of the will of God. Magic aims at commanding or manipulating the supernatural to do the bidding of the magician. It is a desire for power—power to control and direct supernatural or spiritual power. In addition, it is against the will of God. God's intention is that man would obey and trust Him. Seeking to involve oneself with spirits is contrary to God's intention for men.

Satanism. Satanism, although it is not always classed with magic, will be discussed here because it is closely related to black magic.

Satanism is the worship of Satan, a submission of the human will to the will of Satan. Black magic formulas and incantations often contain words of commitment to Satan or spirits. Black magic essentially seeks to use Satan as one might us a tool. All Satanists are involved with black magic, yet not all black magicians are Satanists. A black magician does not necessarily, at least openly, worship Satan as the Satanist does. Black magic uses magical powers for personal ends, while Satanism takes recourse directly to Satan for worship or for obtaining some purely personal end. Nothing is more clearly demonic than Satan worship, but black magic and white magic are actually disguised forms of Satan worship since both involve putting oneself at the disposal of spirits or the devil himself.

FORTUNE-TELLING

Fortune-telling is actually a specialized form of magic. Magic is concerned with power, and fortune-telling is concerned with knowledge. Merrill Unger writes:

---

[8] Ibid, pp. 193, 302–4, 335.

The relation existing between divination and magic is similar to the relation between prophecy and miracle. Divination and prophecy imply special knowledge, magic and miracle special power. In prophecy and miracle the knowledge and power are divine. In divination and magic they are demonic.[9]

Because of the important difference between fortune-telling and magic, fortune-telling is considered separately from magic here.

A number of occult practices fall under the category of fortune-telling or divination.[10] Some of them are astrology, cartomancy (card laying), palmistry, use of rod and pendulum, crystal gazing, and psychometry.

Astrology. Astrology is the most popular form of fortune-telling today. It is the prediction of human character and destiny based on the stars and their constellations. Devoted astrologers consult their horoscopes daily to determine future events and instructions for the living of the present. The astrologer is concerned to learn of the future; he wants knowledge. The demonological principle of knowledge is clearly seen in the occult practice.

Cartomancy. Cartomancy, or use of cards to learn of the future, finds its chief expression today in the tarot. Each tarot card has a meaning and when "thrown" for someone by an expert will supposedly reveal something about the person's future. To be concerned or engaged in the tarot or other forms of cartomancy is to be concerned with knowing the future. The demonic nature of cartomancy is plainly evident as it is viewed from the principle of knowledge.

Chiromancy. Palmistry or chiromancy is the telling of fortunes or the acquiring of knowledge through studying the lines of the hand. Various lines on the hand and the shape and size of fingers and hand are supposed to reveal significant aspects of the future, particularly concerning length of life, success, and marriage. Again palmistry is concerned with knowing the future.

Rod and pendulum. Use of the divining rod or pendulum is not a

---

[9] Unger, op. cit., p. 121.

[10] The terms "fortune-telling" and "divination" are used synonymously.

popular occult activity in America, although the water divining rod, or witching rod, has some history of use in this country. The rod may be used to locate lost articles, springs of water, or areas of the body that are diseased. The pendulum may be used in much the same way as a Ouija board. It may provide yes or no answers to questions or spell out answers according to a prearranged code. Essentially, the divining rod and pendulum are used to acquire knowledge that is not available through ordinary means.

Crystal gazing. Crystal gazing or mirror mantic is another form of fortune-telling. It finds popular expression in the work and predictions of Jeane Dixon of Washington, D. C. As a girl, Jeane Dixon was given a crystal ball by a gypsy woman, and she used it to foretell the future. Crystal balls have been used to diagnose difficult diseases, recover lost objects, and solve crimes. In the main, it is a predicting device. Some occult practitioners use mirrors and rock crystals as well as or in place of crystal balls. The central point, though, in that the crystal ball, mirror, or rock crystal gazer does so to acquire knowledge and thus clearly points up the demonological principle of knowledge.

Psychometry. Psychometry is a form of fortune-telling where the psychometry practitioner holds in his hand an object and then proceeds to make statements about the owner of the object without ever having known or seen the owner. The aim of psychometry is to acquire knowledge not obtainable through ordinary or scientific means.

Fortune-telling principle. Fortune-telling demonstrates a demonological principle, that of knowledge. And to have knowledge of the future is in a sense to have power—over the future.

SPIRITISM

Spiritism is essentially communication with the supposed spirits of the dead. However, supernatural phenomena other than communication with the dead or spirits is commonly included under the heading of spiritism. In spiritism, two principles of demonology are clearly seen: knowledge and power.

Merrill Unger, writing on spiritism, says:

> Modern spiritism is nothing more nor less than ancient

sorcery revival, with particular emphasis on communication with the supported spirits of the dead, which are really deceiving impersonation demons, so that the phenomenon is basically demonism.[11]

Spiritualists like to distinguish between good and bad spirits. They are fond of saying they communicate only with good spirits. Mediums make a show of excluding evil spirits from their séances. They may be sincere but have been deceived into thinking there is a difference between spirits. There is only one Holy Spirit; every other is an evil spirit. The spirits of the spiritualists are demons. There is no question about it.

Necromancy. Necromancy is essentially fortune-telling but could also be classed with spiritism, because it involves communication with the supposed spirits of the dead, or occasionally, spirits from other planets or worlds, and even pre-Adamic beings. Necromancy aims at communicating with the dead, generally for the purpose of acquiring knowledge. This was the case with Saul and the medium at Endor (1Sam. 28:7–25).

An eighteen-year-old girl had been coming regularly to a Bible study class I was teaching. Then she dropped out of sight. Months later I discovered that she had joined a spiritualist church, and her main interest was necromancy. She regularly communicated with a supposed spirit of the dead; she received advice and moral admonitions from the demon. She said the spiritualist church was more spiritual than Christian worship. She liked the idea that her "guide" spirit talked with her, which was something the Holy Spirit had not done.

Her case is nothing new. All over the Bay Area I find this same thing happening. Necromancy does work, but not as a way to talk to the dead; rather, it is a sure way to become demon-possessed.

Other forms of spiritism. Other forms of spiritism—or spiritualism, if it is in a religious context—are spiritistic visions and trances, table-lifting, glass-moving, automatic writing, materializations, astral projection, telekinesis, levitation, and apports (producing a material object at a spiritualist séance without any apparent physical means). Spiritism often combines magic and fortune-telling. This

---

[11] Unger, op. cit., p. 158.

is seen in connection with automatic writing, in which spirits, who are thought to be controlling the head of the writer, will occasionally write out a prediction or answer a question in regard to the future or the unknown. Spiritism, then, in the case of necromancy and other practices mentioned that involve predictions or answers to questions, clearly fits into the demonological principle of seeking to acquire knowledge by other than ordinary means. The mediumistic trances and visions, levitation, apports, materializations, table-lifting, and glass-moving are all known by the spiritist to be accomplished by the agency of power of spirits—spirits of deceased persons, or other spirits or demons. Spiritism essentially seeks to communicate with or dominate the spirit world; it seeks to have power over the supernatural.

DEMONIC POSSESSION

To be possessed by a demon, or to be demonized, commonly means that a person's whole organism and personality are under the control of an invading spirit or demon. But a demon-possessed person does not usually appear possessed and is not always controlled every moment by the indwelling demon. If that were the case, the person would be immediately institutionalized. To say "possessed" is to interpret the work of an indwelling invading spirit or demon; it is safer to use the word "demonized"— a slightly altered transliteration of the New Testament Greek word usually translated "possessed." In this study, the word "demonization" is used to include the term "demon (ic) possession." It may be possible to say a person is demonized, without, however, meaning that the person has actually been indwelt by a demon.

Kurt Koch cites a psychiatrist, Alfred Lechler, who on the basis of his observations distinguished three categories of demonization. They are (1) possession; (2) influence by demons; and (3) deception.[12] Alan Redpath also cite three categories of demonization: (1) oppression and/or depression; (2) obsession; and (3) possession.[13]

---

[12] Kurt Koch, *Christian Counseling and Occultism* (Grand Rapids: Kregel Publications, 1965), p. 217.

[13] Alan Redpath, "Demon Possession Today" in *Victory Over Demonism Today*, Russell Meade (Chicago: Christian Life Publications Inc. 1062,), p. 19.

Doctor Lechler's "influence by demons" is roughly equivalent to Redpath's "oppression and obsession." Demonization then means more than simple demon possession. To be demonized may or may not indicate an indwelling of a person by a demon. Moreover, a person who is indwelt by a demon is not necessarily totally controlled all of the time by the possessing demon.

Psychology has offered a number of explanations for the observable phenomenon of what is referred to as demonic possession. Edward Langton feels that a hypothesis frequently held today is that such possession depends on a person's belief in the power of demons to enter him. The belief in demons is the major factor, according to such a theory: the reality of any demon is quite immaterial. T. H. Gaster writes:

> From the standpoint of religious psychology, demonism represents an externalization of human experiences. Feelings and sensations, moods and impulses, even physical conditions, which might otherwise be described as obtaining autonomously within a man, are portrayed, on this basis, an outer forces working upon him.[14]

Such a view would apply to contemporary possession as well as to cases of possession found in the New Testament. New Testament accounts and many modern accounts of possession are actual instances of real demons demonizing people, Alfred Lechler, on the basis of his own study and psychiatric practice, says, "Possession is neither an outdated Biblical report nor a theological invention but a dreadful reality."[15]

JESUS AND DEMON POSSESSION

The ministry of Jesus to the demonized was discussed in chapter 3, so only a few brief statements are necessary here.

Demonized persons recognized Jesus, and in the case of the Gerasene demoniac Jesus expelled demons so that the possessed might

---

[14] T. H. Gaster, "Demons, Demonology," in *Interpreter's Bible Dictionary*, ed. George A. Buttrick (New York: Abingdon Press, 1962), p. 818. For a detailed account of views of demon possession see: Koch, op. cit., pp. 168–227.

[15] Koch, op. cit., p. 256

become His disciple. Jesus, method of casting out of demons involved no kind of ritual of incantation or conjuration; He simply commanded and the demons obeyed Him. Jesus amazed His contemporaries with His authority over the demons. Ministering to the possessed was a small but significant part of the total ministry of Jesus. He warned His disciple about being overly excited with their authority over evil spirits (Luke 10:20), while at the same time He gave His disciples authority over them. In Acts the disciples expressed this authority by casting demons out of the demonized (Acts 16:18; 19:11–16.). The Synoptic Gospel writers present Jesus as fully believing in demons and their ability to indwell people. Jesus never feared demons or taught fear of demons; He was and remains master over them.

Jesus believed that a person delivered from demon possession could be repossessed. Matthew 12:43–45 records Jesus' important teaching on repossession. He speaks of a man who had one indwelling unclean spirit that was cast out. The spirit sought rest but found none. It returned and found some significant, good changes in the life of the person, but the person was spiritually empty. The demon found seven other spirits, and the eight of them possessed this once-delivered man. It is also significant that, apart from the man (the flesh), the spirit was restless. The main point is that the spiritually empty man was repossessed.

BECOMING DEMON POSSESSED

Voluntary and involuntary possession. It has been the writer's experience that there are two types of demonization: voluntary and involuntary. Voluntary possession refers to a willingness on the part of a person to have demons or spirits enter him. A mediumistic trance is characteristic of a voluntary possession. The possessing spirits are rarely recognized as demons, but the emphasis here is on the willingness of a person to be indwelt. Possession of a person does not mean that a demon completely controls him all of the time; it seems that a demon may reside passively in a person and manifest itself at different times. Involuntary demonization refers to some kind of influence of a person by a demon, perhaps resulting in an obsession, possession, oppression, depression, bizarre behavior, or deception. Demons cannot indwell a person against their will. Therefore, involuntary demonization refers to a person being influenced by the demonic without any conscious or willing yielding to the demonic on his part. Demonization, particularly the indwelling by a demon, can occur only as a person yields to evil spirits or sin.

There is an analogy between a Christian being indwelt by the Holy Spirit and the indwelling of demons. It is clear that possession occurs to people who willingly yield themselves as slaves to demons, either through exposure to the occult, demonic doctrine, or actual Satan worship.

Additional factors. Several factors or conditions may cause exposure to the influence of demons. The occult is the major condition. Demons account for the workability of the occult; to become involved with the occult is to become involved with demons. Yielding to and persisting in sinful activities may expose a person to being demonized. Depression, bitterness, fear, hatred, habitual lust, and greed seem also to bring possible exposure to demons. Raphael Gasson, a former spiritualist medium, says possession can occur during trances, meditation, hypnosis, séances, and involvement in various occult practices.[16] Demons want a passive mind, a blank mind, in a person so that they may make an entrance. Passivity and a blanking out of mental thought and images are very characteristic of many occult practices. Demons are even asked to come and enter into the mind or soul in some occult practices. In black magic and Satanist rituals there are often found actual invitations to evil spirits and/or Satan to take up active residence in a person. Pacts are made, sometimes a blood pact, in which a person gives himself to the devil. Possession commonly occurs under such circumstances.

Koch's four avenues to possession. Kurt Koch offers a convenient summary of the ways in which a person may become demonized:

> Through a great deal of pastoral work I have noticed four ways in which magical powers can originate. These are through heredity, subscription of oneself to the devil, occult experiments, and occult transference.[17]

---

[16] Raphael Gasson, *The Challenging Counterfeit* (Plainfield, N. J.: Logos International, 1966), pp. 82–83.

[17] Kurt Koch, *Between Christ and Satan* (Baden: Evangelization Publishers, 1967), p. 62.

By heredity Koch means the passing on of occult powers or occult involvement from parent to child, aunt to nephew or niece, even through many generations. He says it may be through genes or through a kind of diabolic succession.[18] Subscription to the devil might mean making a pact with the devil or being initiated into an occult group in which there is a giving of oneself over to the group or occult religion. Occult experiments refer to involvement, even casual involvement, in occult practices. Occult transference refers to occult ability —PSI ability—being willingly exchanged between people. (PSI ability refers to para-psychological phenomena like telepathy and clairvoyance.) Transference could mean one person acquiring occult or PSI ability through an initiate receiving a laying on of hands from experienced occultists, or through continued contact with a demon-ized person.

SYMPTOMS OF POSSESSION

There is a wealth of information regarding symptoms of possession; they are observable.

Personality take-over. The chief characteristic of demon pos-session is the projection of a new personality into the possessed. It destroys or temporarily alters the rational structure of the mind. It does the same to the ethical and logical principles of reason.

The take-over of one's personality by an alien force is the most notable feature in all cases of possession. What occurs, then, in demon possession is that the possessed has yielded to or has been taken over by something outside himself, particularly by a demon. The take-over, or possession, is evidenced by a change of personality. The trance state of spiritist mediums and yoga meditations demonstrates most clearly the invasion of a person by a demon.

The trance. The ecstatic trance, as a state of being, is common to demon possession. During a mediumistic trance the medium is whol-ly out of himself, often not remembering what occurred during the trance. In such a trance there is a loss of control over faculties and consciousness.

---

[18] David St. Clair's article, "Psychic Women Reveal Their Weird Powers," in *Journal*, June 1972, discusses six well-known female occultists. It is interest-ing to note that five of the six had relatives who were also occultists.

Occultists have occasionally referred to the "trance" Peter experienced as recorded in Acts 10:9–16 as biblical support for trances experienced in occult practices. The passage reads:

> *The next day, as they were on their journey and coming near the city, Peter went up on the housetop to pray, about the sixth hour. And he became hungry and desired something to eat; but while they were preparing it, he fell into a trance and saw the heaven opened, and something descending, like a great sheet, let down by four corners upon the earth. In it were all kinds of animals and reptiles and birds of the air. And there came a voice to him, "Rise, Peter; kill and eat." But Peter said, "No, Lord; for I have never eaten anything that is common or unclean." And the voice came to him again a second time, "What God has cleansed, you must not call common." This happened three times, and the thing was taken up at once to heaven.*

There are significant differences between the trance or vision Peter experienced and mediumistic trances. Peter did not seek such a state of being, rather it came upon him; there is nothing that might suggest anything like a séance or self-hypnosis. The mediumistic trances, though, are states of being that are actually sought. Peter had no trouble in distinguishing the elements or contents of the trance, whereas the contents of most mediumistic trances are confused and obscure. Peter experienced no fear; he was perplexed as to the meaning of the vision, but he was not alarmed at what he had seen. Mediumistic trances, though, can produce fear and confusion. Peter was fully aware of his conscious being and his religious training which shows he retained his memory and thinking capability; mediumistic trances characteristically involve a sacrifice of the conscious ego state. Peter's trance came from God as evidenced in the conversion of Cornelius, the Roman centurion, of whom the trance spoke. Mediumistic trances do not bring a person to faith and commitment to Christ.

Koch's analysis of the Gerasene demoniac. Kurt Koch analyzed Mark 5:1–15, the account of the Gerasene demoniac, to get at the symptoms of the possessed. His analysis is as follows:

v. 2, possessed with an unclean spirit.

v. 3, accelerated motoric—no one can bind him.

v. 4, paroxysm—he breaks shackles and strikes himself with stones.

v. 6, disintegration—desire for help and fear of help.

v. 7, resistance—defense against Jesus.

v. 7, hyperesthesia—he recognized the deity of Jesus and His plenipotency.

v. 9, psychic variations—change of voice.

v. 12, occult transference—entrance into swine.[19]

Physical symptoms. Physical problems may also be the result of demonic influence.[20] There may also be observable physical conditions associated with possession. The demonized may demonstrate considerable strength—strength far beyond what would seem normal. There may be voice changes, abrupt facial changes, extreme rage and hatred toward anything Christian (especially Jesus and the Bible), violence toward others, mediumistic powers such as clairvoyance and telepathy, and an inability or a struggle to read the Bible, pray, or say aloud the name of Jesus. The closer a possessed person comes to being free of a demon, the more fearful and antagonistic he may become. Fear is one of the major symptoms of demonization. Immorality and abrupt changes in ethical values sometimes goes along with it. Possession may take the form of a physical illness. In the Bible the woman with the "spirit of infirmity" (Luke 13:11–16) and the suppose epileptic by (Matthew 17:14–18 had physical symptoms that were demonic in origin.

Psychic healers are reputed to heal people. There are magicians who "heal" people. This kind of healing is demonic. No real healing has occurred, but rather a demon-possessed person with the demon manifesting itself as an illness experiences a change in the form of the possession. It is very deceiving and convinces people that a mediumistic or magic healer is doing a "good thing."

A precautionary note. It must be stressed that not all of these symptoms in themselves are necessarily an indication of demonization. Some of these symptoms may be manifested in a person who is mentally ill or temporarily confused due to some trauma. Patience and care along with experienced counseling are important in ministering to people who might be demonized.

---

[19] Koch, *Christian Counseling and Occultism*, p. 226.

[20] Matthew 9:32, 33; 12:22; Mark 5:5; 9:17, 18.

RELIEF AND FREEDOM FROM DEMONIC POSSESSION

Relief and freedom from demonic possession or influence are possible because of the work of Jesus Christ. That work is His death on the cross and His resurrection from the dead. With Jesus Christ, the believer has victory over Satan and the demons. The power of the demonic has been broken on the cross and the resurrection. Because of the absoluteness of Christ's victory, it is possible for the believer to apply the principle and fact of that victory in his own life. Satan and the demons are overcome because of the shed blood of Jesus and our testimony to that fact.[21]

STEPS TO RELIEF AND FREEDOM

Relief and freedom from the demonic come through Christ alone. Kurt Koch writes:

> Psychiatrists, psychotherapists, psychologists and the like are not qualified to treat people subjected to magic. Magical subjection is neither a medical nor a psychological problem, but one which concerns faith and the Scriptures. Relief and deliverance are only possible through Christ. It is only when the person subjected to occultism desires to come to Christ that a genuine and complete deliverance is possible.[22]

Repentance. Knowing, then, that through the completed work of Jesus Christ deliverance from demonic power is possible, a person troubled by the demonic can find relief.[23] It is first necessary that a person desiring deliverance turn away from sin—especially turn away from, reject, and renounce any and all involvement in occult practices and reading of occult literature, even ceasing to associate with friends involved in the occult.[24] It is essential that all occult and

---

[21] Revelation 12:11 and 1 John 3:8; 5:4, 5.

[22] Koch, *Between Christ and Satan*, p. 93.

[23] Important references are John 17:15; Ephesians 6:16; Hebrews 2:14; 1 John 3:8; 4:4; 5:18; and Revelation 12:11.

[24] In Acts 19:19 new believers in Christ turned away from their occult practices as demonstrated by a public burning of their magical books.

sin involvement be confessed and repented of. It is not a matter to rush over or take lightly.

Faith. Secondly, it is important for the demonically troubled person to place his faith in Jesus Christ. The person needs to become a Christian, taking a clear, open, and public stand for Jesus. In addition, it is important for the person to endeavor to read the Bible, pray, and seek to be in fellowship with other Christians.

Resisting the devil. Thirdly, the person must actively resist the demonic. Resistance is on the basis of faith. An important principle is found in James 4:7: "Submit yourselves therefore to God. Resist the devil and he will flee from you." The exhortation is to submit oneself to God first. The victory of Jesus Christ can be claimed and accepted by the believer. To submit to God is to abide in Him and His victory. After submitting himself to God, the person is to resist the devil.

Laying on of hands. A demon possessed person will need the help of other believers in dealing with demonic influence or possession. Jesus has given His followers authority over the demons, even the authority (not the power, though, for the power is God's along) to cast demons out of a possessed person.[25] Christians may or may not practice laying on of hands in casting demons out of a possessed person. According to the examples of Jesus and Paul, laying on of hands is not necessary. It is important for Christians to lead a person in a prayer of renouncement and confession.

In my own ministry I usually practice the laying on of hands. A person going through deliverance will tremble and even shake uncontrollably, so a hand on the shoulder is comforting and prevents violent movements. It has been my custom to encourage a person to submit himself to God and resist the devil, while I pray for Jesus to cast the demon out. When a demon begins to manifest itself, fear can grip the minister, particularly when there is screaming. Relaxing in the finished work of Jesus Christ is the minister's best stance. It may take a while but the demon will have to go.

Physical manifestations of deliverance. In the process of ministry to a demon-possessed person there are five physical manifestations that I have observed. A person may scream or shout out in terror. The scream may be the demon or the person; it may be a wailing sort

---

[25] Matthew 10:8; Mark 3:15; 6:13; 16:17; Luke 9:1; 10:17; and Acts 16:18.

of scream. In Phillip's ministry in Samaria, demons came out screaming (Acts 8:7). Second, a person may yawn deeply, or there may be
coughing. Third, there may be vomiting or nausea. In this instance a
mucous-like substance may be vomited; I don't believe such mucous
to be the demon, but its presence is a fairly common occurrence.
Fourth, there may be trembling and shaking, uncontrolled and often
accompanied by a groan. Fifth, there may be moderate or extreme
agitation. This means a rapid speed and movement of the hands and
legs and much movement above. All these physical manifestations are
followed by relief when the deliverance is complete.

Obstacles to deliverance. In ministering to possessed persons,
I have noticed a number of tricks that Satan has used to keep a person under his control. The moment possession occurs, the possessing
demon works to prevent the possibility of its being cast out. Satan is
limited in wisdom and quite bound in approach, so I have been able to
pinpoint sixteen different lies or tricks he uses to escape being ejected.

1. The demon says it will kill the possessed person if it is cast out.

2. The demon says it will kill or harm relatives or friends of the
    possessed and/or the minister.

3. The demon says it will kill the minister.

4. The demon tries to convince the possessed that it is the source of
    good feelings and pleasure, thus these good things will be gone if
    it is cast out.

5. The demon appeals to the victim's sense of fairness by claiming it
    is mean to cast out a demon, for then it would be without a home.

6. The demon tries to convince a person that is so bad God cannot
    possibly love him, so it is better to have the demon since he can't
    have God.

7. The demon tries to convince a person that the sin of having a
    demon is unforgivable or that any forgiveness is impossible
    because possession is blasphemy against the Holy Spirit.

8. The demon says God would not have men tamper with spiritual
    matters such as ordering possessing spirits to leave a person, or it
    says the minister has no authority to cast out demons.

9. The demon tries to make the victim fearful that the deliverance

process will fail, so it is better not to attempt it at all.

10. Because, in the deliverance process, a person may feel nause-ated, cough uncontrollably, or have trouble breathing, the demon will use this physical distress to urge a person to terminate the process.

11. Deliverance may be violent or embarrassing, so the demon tries to convince the possessed that deliverance is therefore too extreme or unnecessary.

12. The demon says that if it is cast out it will haunt and trouble the victim or members of his family, even threatening to possess the children or loved ones or pets.

13. The demon says the deliverance process will make the possessed go insane.

14. The demon says it will embarrass the victim by shouting obsceni-ties and/or making the person perform indecent acts.

15. The demon may try to convince the possessed that it is a good spirit or that the victim should pray for the demon rather than have it cast out.

16. The demon says Jesus cannot cast it out.

These sixteen lies have one thing in common—they are all lies. Jesus tells us that Satan is a liar, the father of lies (John 8:44). The problem is that possessed persons often listen to such lies and believe them. The minister must deal with the lies, but especially deal with the persons listening to the lies. I have encountered these lies and tricks many times, and they are always shallow smoke screens put up by possessing demons. It is important to use God's Word in explain-ing the nature of the lies; some important verses along this line are Matthew 10:1; John 3:16; 8:44; 17:15; Romans 8:35-39; 2 Corinthians 11:14, 15; 2 Thessalonians 3:3; 2 Timothy 1:7; 4:18; 1 John 1:9; 3:8; 4:4, 10, 18; 5:18.

The case of Cynthia amply illustrates the problem of listening to the lies of Satan. Cynthia became possessed at her high school while just a freshman. A girl friend of hers told her fortune through palm reading at a party. Through this fortune-telling episode, Cynthia was introduced to a little group of Satan worshipers that met together on the football field during lunch time. As part of her initiation Cynthia signed a blood pact with Satan, declaring that after seven years Satan could have her soul in exchange for being able to have whatever she wanted during the seven-year period. Sex and animal sacrifice were also a part of it, but Cynthia became possessed at that point.

Some months later, Cynthia confessed Jesus as Savior. She grew rather fast spiritually but would act strangely and spend much of her time in trances. At night, demons would torment her physically. Eventually she came for counseling. The situation was very clear, so we began the deliverance process after one month of counseling sessions. But the deliverance went badly. Cynthia continually believed lie after lie spoken to her by the possessing demons. One session went on for two hours without success. These are the lies that Cynthia believed: (1) deliverance was unfair to the demons being cast out; (2) God would not forgive her; (3) the blood pact could not be broken; (4) the demons would kill her if they were cast out; (5) the demons would kill me if they were cast out; (6) deliverance made her violent, and violence is not Christian; and (7) the demons would not leave.

Cynthia's case is by no means unusual; rather, it is fairly typical. The reason the deliverance went badly was that she believed Satan's lies. Since she believed the lies, the demons were able to grasp a foothold on Cynthia. When she becomes willing to be free, the demons can easily be cast out.

Counseling. Some situations demand comprehensive counseling before any deliverance is possible. Often a person will be fearful of bringing to light involvement in sin and the occult. It may be that several days, or even weeks, will pass before ministry to a demonically troubled person is successful. It is highly unlikely that such a ministry will be effective if the subject is not willing to be freed from demonic influence or possession.[26] In addition, follow-up counseling is important. Deliverance is so dramatic and traumatic that there can be lingering confusion and fear. It is essential for a newly delivered person to be in close fellowship with other Christians.

---

[26] For books containing accounts of demon possession see: Koch's *Christian Counseling and Occultism* and *Between Christ and Satan* and Meade's *Victory Over Demonism Today.*

DEMONIZATION OF THE CHRISTIAN

A common question is whether or not a Christian can be demon-possessed. It is possible for a Christian to suffer from demonic influences, but as to the Christian being possessed or indwelt by a demon, it is not easy to give a clear-cut answer. There is no clear evidence in the New Testament of a Christian or believer being possessed. It is said of Judas that Satan entered into him (Luke 22:3), but it is questionable whether Judas may properly be designated as Christian. There are contemporary Christians who believe both ways. Christians who do not believe that a Christian can be possessed say one can be, however, oppressed by a demon. Those who believe a Christian can be demon-possessed point out that the word "filled" in Acts 2:2—"and it [the Holy Spirit] *filled* all the house where they were sitting"—is the same word used in Acts 5:3 to describe what happened to Ananias—"But Peter said, 'Ananias, why has Satan *filled* your heart to lie to the Holy Spirit?...'"

I have encountered Christians who apparently had become demon-possessed or who, upon their conversion, had not been delivered from previous demon possession. There is always a question whether a person who appears to be possessed and claims to be a Christian is actually one; his testimony may be the only supporting evidence for his claim. Of course, it may be that a Christian who appears possessed is actually suffering from some form of mental illness or temporary confusion and/or depression. Yet, it is possible for a Christian—due to rebellion, hardness of heart, desire to experience sin, or ignorance— to come under the influence of the demonic. It has been my experience that Christians have become demon-possessed through involvement with the occult or by harboring and entertaining sin or a desire for sin. In my ministry to Christians who have been demon-possessed I have noticed that it is common for the demon to hide in order to escape detection. But when a believer starts to grow and draw close to Jesus, the demon will become more active and noticeable. Deliverance of a demon-possessed Christian is nearly always simple and sure. They are much stronger and effective after deliverance.

Certainly Christ protects from Satan those who trust Him and are resisting the devil. Good evangelical Bible scholars stand on both sides of this question. After careful examination of the Bible I cannot find substantial support for either position. One church I knew experienced a split in the fellowship over the issue—this should not be divisive. Let us not be the judge in such an issue but rather deal with each individual situation as God sends it to us. In ministry to people who are suffering from some type of demonism, our ministry should not so much conform to rigid doctrine as it should seek to bring the freedom of Christ to those whom Satan has bound.

DISCUSSION QUESTIONS

1. Describe the essence of magic. What principles particularly relate to magic? How may a Christian keep all traces of magic from his faith and worship?

2. Are the white magic enchantments similar to some forms of worship you have known? Pick out the magical elements in the enchantments recorded in this chapter.

3. Describe the difference and similarities between white, neutral, and black magic and Satanism.

4. How does fortune-telling differ from magic? What are the fortune-teller and the magician hoping to gain?

5. What does it mean to be demon-possessed? Give practical examples of demon influence other than demon possession.

6. Was demonology a major aspect of Jesus' ministry? Explain your answer. How does Luke 10:20 indicate Jesus' attitude toward the demonic?

7. How may a person become demon-possessed? What happens to a person when he becomes possessed?

8. Describe the major symptoms of demon possession. Are there explanations for such symptoms other than demon possession? Explain.

9. Consider these situations: (1) You encounter a person who admits he is demon-possessed: (2) you encounter a person who is involved in the occult but does not believe he is demon-possessed; (3) you encounter a person who is obviously demon-possessed but refused help. How would you minister in each situation?

10. Is it frightening to think that a Christian could be demon-possessed? How may we as Christians keep this issue from becoming divisive?

The devil's cleverest wile is to convince us that he does not exist.

BAUDELAIRE

Satanism is on the rise, because belief in Jesus is growing. The devil is also making his pitch.

BILLY GRAHAM

6
Christianity Versus the Occult

The occult stand in opposition to biblical Christianity, and not syn-thesis is possible. This chapter deals with the conflict between the occult and the Christian faith. It is also concerned with how Christians may witness to people involved with the occult. Because the satanic establishment exists and touches the lives of so many, the Christian has both the opportunity and command to bring the truth and light of Jesus Christ to bear on the deceitfulness of the demonic.

CONFLICT BETWEEN THE OCCULT AND THE CHRISTIAN FAITH

MANIPULATION OF THE SUPERNATURAL

Magic clearly depicts an essential difference between the occult and the Christian faith. Magic is an attempt to manipulate, direct, or con-trol God, spirits, and/or spiritual power. Speaking of the magician, Merrill Unger says, "He prostitutes God's holy name for an unworthy purpose. God is not a handyman who obeys when the magic charmer commands."[1] And again he says, "Viewed from a biblical perspective, this is basic rebellion of the Satanic variety, aiming to have God at one's disposal."[2]

A Time magazine article on the occult pointed out this essential distinction between the occult and the Christian faith, saying, "In Christianity the Gospel message is submission to God; in the occult

---

[1] Merrill F. Unger, *Demons in the World Today* (Wheaton, Ill.: Tyndale House Publishers, 1971), p. 136.

[2] Ibid, p. 141.

the ruling motive is control."[3] Arthur Lyons, a non-Christian, in a book dealing with the resurgence of Satanism and the occult into American life, said that magic "is not supplication, but an attempt at manipulation of universal forces that must obey the practitioner."[4]

Magic is concerned with power. It assumes that with the aid of knowledge and the use of magical rituals, incantations, and spells, a magician can actually bring spiritual forces under his control. The so-called white magic, which purports to deal with good spirits, angels, and even God for benevolent purposes, still clearly involves the control, directions, and manipulation of spiritual forces. In white magic the idea is to compel God or other spiritual forces to act. Even the prayers used in white magic, the name of God, phrases incorporating the names of the Trinity, and biblical quotations are used only by way of a technical formula or tool.

The magician thinks he is controlling supernatural power, but actually the demonic power is controlling the magician. One male witch I met in San Francisco enjoyed his power over women. We were talking on the street, in San Francisco's North Beach District. It was cold but he was barefoot. He viciously attacked Jesus in a loud voice; he said he had more power than Jesus. The devil, he said, was his friend, who gave him all the sex he wanted. Wanting to prove his power, he called a number of girls to him and began to molest them in various ways. They were all a part of his "family," and they followed him blindly. I tried to speak to the girls, and they would swear and spit and give me the traditional hand gestures meaning "praise Satan."

Christian prayer, on the other hand, is an act of submission to the will of God. Jesus said, "Thy will be done."[5] Christ's instruction on prayer clearly points out that the believer is to ask or petition the Father.[6] The believer is not told to command the Father; even the sincere prayer of a righteous man does not make God answer the prayer. God is sovereign and is beyond the control of any man or group. The angels of God, ministering spirits though they be, are not at the beck

---

[3] "The Occult: A Substitute Faith," *Time*, 19 June, 1972, p. 67.

[4] Arthur Lyons, *The Second Coming* (New York: Dodd, Mead & Co., 1970), p. 14.

[5] Matthew 6:10b.

[6] Matthew 6:8; 7:7; John 14:13; 15:17, 16; 16:23; James 1:5.

and call of man. It is clear that God hears the prayer of the believer, but it is never suggested in the Bible that men should pray to angels. Angels minister only at the direction of God and never act contrary to the truth that is in Jesus Christ.[7]

Jesus' action of appointing and sending out the twelve disciples points up the difference between manipulation and submission. Mark, in reporting the instance, says, "And he appointed twelve, to be with him, and to be sent out to preach and have authority to cast out demons."[8] It is authority—not power—that Jesus gave His disciples over the demons. The distinction between authority and power is significant. The power did not reside in the disciples; it is God's alone. The disciples were given authority—authority backed up by the power of God. The disciples were not allowed to perform spiritual manipulations, they had no power over demons, and even their authority depended upon their faith and prayer.[9]

ESP practitioners soon learn to be jealous of the power they have. The problem is that they often believe ESP is a natural or neutral phenomenon. One man I know, who is active in ESP, has the ability to heal people. With the aid of what he calls his "helper" he concentrates on a sick person and then directs "white light" at them. In many instances healings have followed. He claims the power is godly, so he is unwilling to abandon the practice. Member of his church (he is a Christian leader) have pointed out the demonic nature of the healings, but the man is unwilling to lose the power. Another member of the church also has ESP power, and the two are attracting other Christians. They are trying hard to convince people that ESP is "neutral." ESP is real, it works— but it works because Satan and his demons are behind it.

The occult practitioner desires to manipulate the supernatural for his own purpose. The Christian desires to submit himself to God so that the will of God might be accomplished in him.

FAITH VERSUS SIGHT

Faith is a central concept of Christianity. The Christian is to submit to, have faith in, believe, trust, and obey God. Christian faith is more

---

[7] Galatians 1:8.
[8] Mark 3:14, 15. Also see Matthew 10:1; Mark 6:7; and Luke 9:1, 2.
[9] Mark 9:14–29.

than merely intellectually acknowledging the existence, or even the truth, of God.[10] Christian faith has to do with acceptance of, reliance upon, yielding to, and submission to God and His Word. The believers' desire is to do the will of God.

The occultist, however, recognizes spirits, spirit power, demons, and even God without yielding to or submitting to God and His Word. The occult concentrates on phenomena, having spirit-power accomplish something. It is physical in nature and not actually spiritual. The occultist seeks proofs and wonders; he wants comfort and assurance. It is just such seeking that draws many people into the occult. They are eager, with and evil fascination, to glimpse or experience spiritual things.

Middle class occultism is religious, that is, it has the appearance of spirituality. Most Christians I have known who have involved themselves in some kind of occult practice object to any criticism of it and point out its spiritual nature. This is particularly true of Christians involved in yoga, mind awareness, or meditation groups. They usually talk of how much value they are receiving from it. One man said he was finding more spirituality in his yoga group than in his church. He argued strongly for yoga, pointing out how well the yoga master spoke of God. He was actively recruiting members of his church for the class. He did not realize the way he had been deceived by Satan. He was becoming an evangelist for the devil.

The occultist wants sight, signs, and wonders. He is opposed to repentance of sin and submitting type of faith in Jesus Christ. Paul warned that Satan would perform signs and wonders; "The coming of the lawless one by the activity of Satan will be with all power and with pretending signs and wonders...."[11] Jesus warned that false Christs and prophets would also show great signs and wonders.[12] The occult is sight-centered; it is physical, sensual, and feeling-oriented. Much of it is concentrated on the feelings or emotions directly, whereas God ministers to the mind and spirit of man directly. The feelings or emotions of the believer are secondary in importance, although they are to be taken seriously and not denied. God ministers to the whole man

---

[10] James 2:19.

[11] 2 Thessalonians 2:9.

[12] Matthew 24:24.

and not to just a part (i.e., the emotions or senses). A sound Christian principle is to live by faith and not by sight or feelings.[13]

A minister's wife was fond of telling others of the miraculous things that had happened to her. She had had visions that foretold future events accurately. She was warned of a death in the family that came to pass. At a meeting I heard her describing her experiences. She wanted everyone to know that miracles do indeed occur today—but the miracles were of a questionable nature. She was encouraging people to seek for visions and dreams. Nowhere in the Bible is the believer encouraged to seek for such visions and prophetic dreams. If evangelism does not directly point to Jesus, it is not Christian evangelism.

OCCULT PASSIVITY VERSES CHRISTIAN ACTIVITY

Achieving a passive state of mind is essential to many forms of the occult. This is especially true of spiritualism, mediumistic hypnosis, telepathy, mind reading, and practices associated with séances. In fact, passivity plays an extremely important role in the occult. It has been the writer's experience that states of passivity allow a demon access to the personality. It seems that a passive state of mind is conducive, if not essential, to demon possession.

Closely akin to a passive state of mind is focusing or concentrating on a single object, concept, or mental image. One yoga class of which I knew concentrated on the word "Jesus." Everything was blocked out except the word "Jesus." That is not Christian—it is demonic. The Christian is never told to concentrate on the name or word "Jesus." In some occult practices, religious-type chants or mantras are recited over and over. Such chanting can bring a person into a condition like that of the passive side of the mind. It is similar to self-induced hypnosis. Yoga and transcendental meditation particularly use chants and physio-psychological exercises to "clear" the mind of active thought, worries, frustrations, and similar feelings. Usually matter and flesh are viewed as evil or detrimental to the reception of spiritual or psychical impressions.

Bhakti-yoga is a form of mediation identical to astral-travel or projection. A. C. Bhaktivedanta, Swami, head of the International Society of Krishna Consciousness, is America's foremost teacher of

---

[13] Romans 1:17; 2 Corinthians 5:7.

bhakti-yoga. He asserts that the devotee can journey to other planets, planets that are spiritual and where life is eternal and blissful. This form of yoga relies on the use of chants and mantras. In the passive state of mind (or trance), demonic forces deceive the devotee into thinking he is traveling to other planets. Satan twists and manipulates the mind of a person in a trance, but it all has a sense of the supernatural about it.

The Christian is never encouraged to adopt or seek to achieve passive states of mind. Quite to the contrary, we are encouraged toward an active expression of the whole being to God. Christian worship is an active expression of praise, adoration, and thanksgiving, and it is always directed and purposeful worship, that is, it is always directed toward God. Christian prayer is an active expression of the thoughts, needs, and intents, and praises of the believer to God. The Bible does not view the flesh and mind of man as evil, nor does the Bible indicate the flesh and mind of man are obstacles that must be put aside or circumvented.

There is a kind of mediation, though, that is biblical. It is meditation that does not seek or involve passivity. Biblical meditation centers on God, His Word, His law, His wondrous work of creation, but it is clear that it is not in any sense passive. Biblical meditation is active. For example, the psalmist says, "... And on his law he meditates day and night."[14] Again the psalmist said, "I will mediate on all thy works...."[15] Biblical meditation, then, is active and directed to, or centered in, God.

THE DANGER OF THE OCCULT

The large number of people participating in contemporary occult practices is indicative of the tremendous drawing power of the demonic. The occult fascinates; it has a strong but subtle charm, an evil charm really, that at least arouses the curiosity. It works and it is dangerous. I have often witnessed the destructiveness of the occult. Probably the most dangerous aspect of the demonic is that many Christians who are ignorant of it hazards become involved. My experience has shown that ESP, astrology, mind dynamics or yoga-meditation groups are

---

[14] Psalm 1:2b.

[15] Psalm 77:12. Also see Psalms 5:1; 19:14; 49:3; 63:6; 104:34; 119:15, 23, 48, 78, 97, 99.

Satan's main tools for deceiving the Christian. The devil is no respect-er of persons.

GENERAL HARMFUL CHARACTERISTICS OF THE OCCULT

Kurt Koch, who has had wide pastoral experience with people involved in the occult, makes the following analysis of the conse-quences of magic. He says,

> For it is an empirical fact of pastoral care that where white and black magic are practiced, there we have psychic distur-bances in the family. The rule may have exceptions, although I have met with no exceptions where there were active occult-ists.[16]

As to fortune-telling, Koch states that two typical characteristics of the consequences of the occult practice are depression and a loss of moral inhibition.[17]

In general consideration of people involved in the occult, Koch says, "The characteristics of such people reveal abnormal passions, instability, violent tempers, addiction to alcohol, nicotine, and sexual vices, selfishness, gossiping, egotism, cursing, etc."[18]

Adolph Koberle, in the introduction to Koch's book, Christian Counseling and Occultism, speaks of people who had been involved in some form of the occult and came to Doctor Koch for counseling.

> The person did, to be sure, find something of a satisfaction for the inquisitiveness, but they always had to pay dearly in the form of psychic affliction of all kinds, such as moods of depression, ennui, suicidal thoughts, blasphemous urges, mania of lascivious compulsions.[19]

---

[16] Kurt Koch, Christian Counseling and Occultism (Grand Rapids: Kregel Pub-lications, 1965), p. 126.

[17] Kurt Koch, Between Christ and Satan (Grand Rapids: Kregel Publications, 1968), p. 31.

[18] Ibid, p. 49.

[19] Koch, Christian Counseling and Occultism, p. 5.

It has been my experience that one of the central consequences of occult involvement is fear. It is fear in general, fear of the dark, of other people, of being alone, of certain books or foods or places, and many nameless fears. Very regularly, sexual indulgence and perversions are also associated with occult involvement. Drug abuse, everything from marijuana to alcohol, is involved. Suicidal thoughts and attempts at suicide are common. A person involved in the occult will generally withdraw into the occult environment, but he may also attempt to bring new people into it. Occultists can be quite missionary-minded, particularly when a financial profit is to be made through sales of books, membership fees, and similar activities.

The following cases from my own ministry demonstrate some of the consequences of occult involvement:

(1) A high school boy learned simple witchcraft techniques; He began to experience magical powers over the other people and situations. Throughout his occult involvement Christians spoke with him and told him about Jesus; he attended several Bible studies but was never able to sit through a single one. After some months he renounced his witchcraft and became a Christian. However, he continued to suffer from fear that was often vague and undefined. After several months his fearfulness left him.

(2) A group of Satanists cast a spell on a Christian youth group. It caused fear in the group. The fear was such that they were undergoing some strain and loss of purpose.

(3) A Christian girl became involved with telepathy through the influence of her boyfriend. She began suffering from fear and a deterioration of her Christian faith. The boy was able to break into her thoughts and actually communicate with her, even against her will.

(4) A young high school girl began experimenting in the occult. Her resultant bizarre behavior brought her to the attention of her friends, some of whom were Christians. These friends succeeded in bringing her to a Bible study, where she made a profession of faith in Jesus. Within a short time she moved away and could find no Christian fellowship. She slipped back into the occult and began rejecting Jesus and the Bible, all the while becoming more and more disoriented and withdrawn.

(5) A stout, middle-aged woman appeared at a Bible study one evening. She was unable to relate how it was that she learned

about the study. During counseling afterward, she told of long occult involvement, especially with astrology, palm reading, and spiritualism. Every night an incubus, a demon appearing in a male form, would have sexual relations with her. She reported having a guide spirit that spoke regularly with her. She was very fearful and had strong suicidal thoughts. However, she declined any help and the offer of further counseling.

(6) A college girl, a pretty and bright student, began experimenting with witchcraft. It led her into immorality and confusion about life. She began having suicidal thoughts and was always either confused or afraid. After renouncing her witchcraft and sin, she began to improve almost immediately.

THE MYSTERY OF THE OCCULT

Part of the danger of the demonic is that it is extremely hard to get a clear intellectual grasp of it. Even the biblical record does not answer all our questions, particularly in regard to extrasensory perception and other contemporary psychic phenomena. There is much that is unexplainable. The phenomenon sometimes referred to as "neutral telepathy," for example, presents a great difficulty. Is there a means of unconscious or subconscious communication? There seems to be a kind of intuition that operates between two people who have intimate knowledge of each other. Many people have experienced what might be called "intuition." But neutral telepathy seems to be a step beyond "normal intuition"—perhaps a dangerous step beyond it. The problem comes in distinguishing the so-called neutral telepathy from the occult practice of "mental" telepathy. If there is a difference between the two, it may be only academic, so that in actual practice the two may actually blur or lead one into the other. "Mental" telepathy itself is mediumistic and definitely classed with the occult.

A minister who lives near me professes to be an expert on demonology. He claims and preaches that ESP is "neutral"; he means that it is unexplainable but definitely not demonic. Consequently, some people who have believed his word began experimenting with ESP and thereby exposed themselves to demons. The problem is that the minister himself is able to read minds and does not want to think that he has been deceived by Satan. When pressed to explain it, he says his "gift" is just a very sensitive intuitive power. But he has compromised the truth and is hurting those to whom he ministers.

The demonic cannot be fully understood by man. Paul spoke of "the mystery of iniquity." Demons are not little, ugly-looking dwarfs dressed in red, yet it is far easier to describe what they are not than what they are. They are mysterious, and their power and influence are shrouded. In contrast to the difficulty of closing in on the mystery of the occult, Christian ministry to the demonized has provided immediate, healthy results. In the midst of uncertainty about the demonic, the Bible provides a very useful principle. Paul says in Romans 14:23, "... For whatever does not proceed from faith is sin." And the "faith" is faith centered in Jesus Christ.

ANTI-CHRISTIAN NATURE OF THE OCCULT

The occult clearly leads a person away from biblical faith in Jesus Christ. This may take the form of meditation-plus-Jesus, or using Edgar Cayce's or Jeane Dixon's books for devotional reading. Occult commitment demands a rejection of Jesus Christ (religion is not rejected), and acceptance of biblical Christianity demands a rejection of the occult.

Victor Ernest, a former spiritualist, notes that the job of demons is to lead people away from dependence on God. He declares they are doing this through spiritualist churches, séances, psychic phenomena, witchcraft, and idol worship.[20]

One of the more cleaver devices of Satan I've seen recently is the best-selling book by Richard Bach called *Jonathan Livingston Seagull*. Bach "received" the story, that is, a voice spoke it to him. The author, a former Christian Scientist, has been involved with mediums, especially with Jane Roberts. The book seems very spiritual and many have considered it Christian-oriented. But in my counseling ministry I have seen that it has had harmful effects. It teaches self-reliance, perfection, and a definite form of "works" religion. It also teaches a kind of God-consciousness typical of Hindu thought. I believe it is a demon-inspired book and that the "voice" Bach has listened to is a demon.

Koch helpfully presents the anti-Christian nature of the occult practices. He says:

---

[20] Victor Ernest, *I Talked With Spirits* (Wheaton, Ill.: Tyndale House Publishers, 1970), p. 18.

In spite of arguments of the contrary counseling confirms that fact that when a Christian gets involved in any form of spiritistic activity his spiritual life can be seriously affected. This is not true for the Buddhist or the Moslem or the followers of other religions like this. These religions are not impaired by spiritism. But spiritism does immunize people against the working of the Holy Spirit. We must be clear in our minds about the distinction here. A person's religious life is not harmed by occultism or spiritism. Indeed spiritism itself is to a large extent a 'religious' movement. The devil does not take away our 'religiousness,' his real desire is to sever us from Christ and to prevent us from following Him.[21]

Two of the principles of biblical demonology have to do with power and knowledge. Gaining power and knowledge through the occult give a person a "spiritual" feeling or sense and, consequently, leads away from godly spirituality.

THE OCCULT AS A COUNTERFEIT

Many occultists claim to be Christians. They may claim that their practice is Bible-centered. Spiritualists in particular present their group as just another of the many religious (even Christian) denominations. They often incorporate Bible reading, hymn singing, and prayer into their services. Jeane Dixon makes use of her Catholic background and claims that God is the source of her power and predictions. Betty Bethard, a psychic healer in California, makes considerable use of her Baptist background and considers herself a Christian performing a helpful ministry.

The occult may seem to be a good and religious practice, particularly as it becomes more socially acceptable. However, be it ever so spiritual it can only approximate or simulate the real person and ministry of the Holy Spirit. Because of its cleaver guise the occult deceives many sincere seekers after truth and God. Occult worship is quite soulful in nature—emotional, inspirational, feeling-centered. Some Christian groups worship in ways that are emotion-centered; they may experience what seem to be spiritual blessings but are actually

---

[21] Koch, *Between Christ and Satan*, op. cit., p. 124.

quite soulful. Watchman Nee, in the *Latent Power of the Soul,* warns against the possibility of Christians experiencing soulful rather than spiritual worship. I have personally encountered many groups whose "deep" spiritual worship consisted of entering into trance-like state of bliss. This is far too close to the occult for comfort and is especially identifiable with spiritualism, group mind control, and transcendental meditation. In one such meeting the leader rocked back and forth with his eyes closed saying, "Jesus, Jesus," over and over. Two girls spent almost one hour with the hands raised, eyes closed, and mouths open. It looked vaguely spiritual but was actually counterfeit worship.

EXTREME APPROACHES TO THE OCCULT

C. S. Lewis, in the preface to his *Screwtape Letters,* clearly expresses extreme approaches to demons and the occult.

There are two equal and opposite errors into which our race can fall about the devils. One is to disbelieve in their existence. The other is to believe, and to feel and excessive and unhealthy interest in them. They themselves are equally pleased by both errors and hail a materialist or a magician with the same delight.[22]

Karl Barth had a similar thought in mind when he said:

If we ignore demons, they deceive us by concealing their power until we are again constrained to respect and fear them as powers. If we absolutize them, respecting and fearing them as true powers, they have deceived us by concealing their character as falsehood, and it will be only a little while before we try to ignore and are thus deceived by them again.[23]

The Bible neither overemphasizes nor dismisses the demonic. Biblical Christianity has a healthy view of demons. Even a systematic study of the satanic may not be extremely healthy and can have deleterious effects upon the researchers. It is not necessary for Christians to understand the occult thoroughly; after reading a manual such as this, most believer have enough information on it. I have known a number of Christians to develop an unhealthy interest in the occult.

---

[22] C. S. Lewis, *Screwtape Letters* (New York: The Macmillan Co., 1956), p. 9.

[23] Karl Barth, *Church Dogmatics,* ed. G. W. Bromiley and T. F. Torrance, 4 vols. (Edinburgh: T. and T. Clark, 1936—62), 3:526–27.

The demonic needs to be understood, respected for its pseudo power but, never appreciated or feared.

CHRISTIAN RESPONSE TO PEOPLE AND GROUPS INVOLVED WITH THE OCCULT

The Church of Jesus Christ is the only institution able to deal success-fully with the demonic. The Christian has a position on the occult; he has firm ground on which to stand. The Christian knows that Jesus Christ stands as Lord over

> *all rule and authority and power and domination, and above every name that is named, not only in this age but also in that which is to come; and he has put all things under his feet and has made him the head over all things for the church, which is his body, the fullness of him who fills all in all.*[24]

The Christian must recognize that he is not an exorcist, in com-petition with magicians. Magicians perform exorcisms, but Christians simply acknowledge that it is Jesus Christ alone who has power to cast out demons. We Christians stand with and in Jesus Christ, hum-bly recognizing that Christ will work His work in us as we minister to the demonized. Christian response to the occult is simply the procla-mation and the ministering of the truth of the Gospel of Jesus Christ.

Many times my friends and I have confronted groups involved in demonic practices. We have often handed out literature to people on their way into a meeting of occultists. We have conducted Chris-tian witnessing in front of occult bookstores. And people have been converted at such times. Many Christians, ignorantly participating in occult groups, have been successfully warned through such evange-lism. Christians must meet the occult challenge head-on. The devil is aggressive, and the Christian community must not be passive in their witness. The Apostle Peter said, "Your adversary the devil prowls around like a roaring lion, seeking some one to devour."[25]

Toleration of the occult is useless. Compromise with the occult can be disastrous. Participation in the occult is sin. God has already judged it as such, and regardless of contemporary views of the occult,

---

[24] Ephesians 1:21–23.

[25] 1 Peter 5:8.

God's judgment stands.[26] The Christian may view the occult as another form of sin and view the occultist as a sinner for whom Jesus died. In my experience with occultists, I have found that a firm, biblical loving approach has been most successful. The word or counsel that brings freedom is repentance to God and faith in our Lord Jesus Christ.[27] Many times it has been helpful to lay hands on a demonized person and cast the demon out, after having explained the Gospel and the necessity of turning away from all contact with the occult. In Christ, Christians have sure victory over Satan and demons.

When I began writing this manual, a verse from Martin Luther's hymn, "A Mighty Fortress is Our God," seemed to be a perfect ending to such a work on demonology. It still does. Luther wrote:

> And tho' this world, with devils filled,
> Should threaten to undo us;
> We will not fear, for God has willed
> His truth to triumph through us.

DISCUSSION QUESTIONS

1. What are the differences between faith and magic? Why is it wrong for the Christian to try to command or manipulate God?

2. How might the occult seem more "here and now" to some people then Christianity? Distinguish between the spirituality of Christianity and the sensuality of the occult.

3. What is wrong with the passive state of mind? Distinguish between Christian meditation and yoga meditation.

4. List the possible results of participating in the occult. Why might a person involved in fortune-telling be fearful?

5. In what way is the occult mysterious? What does a Christian need to understand about the occult?

---

[26] See Leviticus 19:26, 31; 20:27; Deuteronomy 18:9–12; Isaiah 2:6;Acts 19:18; Galatians 5:20; Revelation 21:8; 22:15.

[27] Acts 20:21. Paul's ministry to the Ephesians was quite successful, especially his ministry to occultists living in Ephesus, as recorded in Acts 19:18, 19. Paul's words as found in Acts 20:21 were addressed to the Ephesian elders.

6. Is it possible to be involved in an occult practice and still be a Christian? Why?

7. How can the occult be religious and not be Christian?

8. What kind of strategy might Christians adopt that would effectively confront occultists with the freedom that is in Jesus Christ?

9. Compile a list of Bible verses that describe Christ's victory over Satan and that assure the Christian of that same victory in his own life and ministry.

Appendix A
Selected Demonological
Terms and Definitions

AMULET. An amulet is an object said to have magical power or significance. The object is worn or carried on the person. Usually there is an inscription or picture on the amulet that has magical significance. Common inscriptions are a goat's head, star, horseshoe, tail of a fox, mandrake root, lizard, fingernail, key, knot, scorpion, or magic words or phrase. An amulet might be intended to provide protection, insure success, or even cause harm to persons. A charm, talisman, or fetish might also be used as an amulet.

APPARITION. An apparition is the appearance of a disembodied or ghostlike form. In mediumistic circles, an apparition may look and speak like a deceased person. Apparitions are usually transparent, have the appearance of being clothed, and seem to be white or yellowish in color.

APPORT. An apport is the appearance and/or disappearance of a physical object in a closed room usually with the aid of a medium and without the aid of any physical agent.

ASTRAL PROJECTION. Astral projection is the partial or complete separation of the so-called astral body (soul) from the physical body, and the traveling (projection) to other places in the physical or spiritual realm. Such traveling or excursion of the soul may occur during sleep or while in a trance. The "spiritual" voyage may or may not be recalled at the conclusion of the trance or sleep. The practiced astral projectionist is said to be able to visit wherever or whatever he wishes. Astral projection can be used as a form of fortune-telling; it is often the goal of meditation.

ASTROLOGY. Astrology is a form of fortune-telling based on the supposed influences and positons of the stars, moon, sun, and planets upon human affairs. These include predicting terrestrial events by charting the positions and movements of heavenly bodies.

AUGURY. Augury is fortune-telling by means of interpreting omens, portents, entrails of animals, patterns of tea leaves, flight of birds, casting lots or dice, or by chance phenomena.

AUTOMATIC WRITING. Automatic writing is the writing of words without awareness or conscious physical effort. Such writing may occur during a trance. The result is a message or prediction believed to have come from the spirit world through the direct agency of spirits. It is a form of fortune-telling. Automatic writing is different from handwriting analysis.

BLACK MASS. A black mass is celebrated in honor of the devil. Such a mass is commonly celebrated during a witch's sabbath, conducted in the open air traditionally, usually at night (midnight), and the altar is the back or stomach of a naked woman. It is intended to be the reverse or opposite of the Christian (Catholic) Mass; it is intended to be a worship of Satan.

BLOOD PACT. A blood pact is a pact or contract made with Satan. , signed with the blood of the contractee. It may be referred to as an inscription of a person to the devil. Blood pacts may be a part of a black mass or a part of a black magic ritual.

CARTOMANCY. Cartomancy is fortune-telling by means of cards. It is often called card-laying. The cards may be ordinary playing cards or a specialized deck like the tarot. The cards are interpreted along set lines or at the whim of the fortune-teller.

CHARMING. Charming involves the employment of magic. It may be referred to as bewitching, enchanting, becharming, casting spells, and conjuring. It attempts to use spirit power to obtain certain results such as the healing (and diagnosing) of diseases in humans and animals, discovering the whereabouts of lost articles (treasures, persons, water, for example), providing protection against danger or misfortune, or causing harm. It is an attempt to control spiritual power.

CLAIRAUDIENCE. Clairaudience is a spiritualistic faculty for hearing voices, sounds, or words that are not normally heard by others at the same time and under the same circumstances. Such voices, sounds, or words often contain messages or predictions concerning the future, or reveal knowledge not obtainable through ordinary means. The phenomenon is used by occultists to substantiate a spirit world that supposedly is benevolent.

CLAIRSENTIENCE. Clairsentience is the spiritualistic diagnosis of diseases without the use of scientific medical diagnostic techniques. It is supposedly spirit-given knowledge of diseases, but it can mean the perception of something beyond that which is not normally perceptible.

CLAIRVOYANCE. Clairvoyance is the spiritualistic ability of discerning things not normally present to the senses. It supposedly enables one to see objects or persons across great distances. It also refers to the mediumistic ability to see spirits or see into the spirit world.

CONJURE. To conjure is to call up the deceased, spirits (good, neutral, or evil), and/or the devil or demons. Various forms of magic are used in conjurations.

COVEN. In witchcraft, a coven is a community of witches generally consisting of six males, six females, and a high priest of priestess.

CRYSTAL GAZING. Crystal gazing includes crystal ball gazing, mirror gazing, and rock crystal gazing. It is a form of fortune-telling whereby messages from the spirit world supposedly appear in visual form in the ball, mirror, or rock crystal.

DIVINATION. Divination is another name for fortune-telling. It intends to gain knowledge of future or otherwise unknown events. Some forms of divination are crystal gazing, astrology, cartomancy, augury, necromancy, and chiromancy.

ECTOPLASM. (Katie, you may want to add: "Ectoplasm is...")An unknown substance that has been used to describe a white, foggy, kind of material which has often been observed to "ooze" from the body of a medium. This unusual substance has been photographed by people engaged in psychical research. It can assume various shapes. It is a substance used by demons in their manifestations.

ENCHANTING. See Charming.

EXTRASENSORY PERCEPTION. Extrasensory perception (ESP) refers to sensing, knowing, or perceiving beyond ordinary or normal means. It should not be confused with intuition which is quite natural, rather infrequent, and non-spiritual. Intuition depends on the conscious or subconscious association or bringing together of seemingly unrelated data to form a picture or bring insight. ESP depends upon extranormal forces, spiritual forces, that are

demonic in nature. ESP may include clairvoyance, telepathy, telekinesis, levitation, apparitions, apports, and materialization.

EXORCISM. Exorcism is the casting out of spirits (good, neutral, or
evil) or Satan from a person so possessed. Exorcism is more a spiritualist than a Christian or biblical term. It may also refer to the
expulsion of demonic spirits or ghosts from places and/or objects.
Spells, incantations, conjurations, and white magic prayers may be
used in exorcisms.

FAMILIAR SPIRIT. In spiritualistic circles, a familiar or guide spirit
is said to be a helping or good spirit that can provide help, information, guidance concerning the future, general spiritual knowledge, comfort, or discernment. Magicians, sorcerers, and witches
may refer to their familiar or guide spirits which make their occult
practice possible.. Many occultists seek familiar spirits to be with
them or indwell them. Many Christians believe that Satan assigns
a demon to every person; this demon is able to learn much of all
there is to know about a person. It is held that this is the spirit that
is talking to during a séance. Because it is so intimately acquainted
with the dead person, it provides a very convincing imitation of the
deceased since it has knowledge of events that only the deceased
could have known.

FORTUNE-TELLING. See Divination.

GUIDE SPIRITS. See Familiar Spirit.

HYPNOSIS. The use of hypnosis and suggestion is not confined to the
scientific (medical and psychological) sphere. It is also used in
occult practices. A hypnotic state resembles sleep but is different
in that it is brought on by the use of suggestion and other opera-
tions of the hypnotizer. The hypnotic subject, while in the hypnotic
trance, remains in rapport with the hypnotizer and even becomes
vulnerable or responsive to suggestions or commands of the hypnotizer. A person in a hypnotic trance is much less capable of ward-
ing off the demonic than he is when in a normal state of mind. It
may be that the use of hypnosis can be justified in determining a
diagnosis, but its use is questionable since it may be viewed as an
invasion into the personality of a man. However, hypnosis is occasionally used by occultists for various purposes, and as such it is
simply an occult or demonic tool.

INCANTATION. An incantation is a spell or charm used in or as a part of a ritual of magic. It may be defined also as a formula of words—spoken, chanted, or sung—that are used for their special magical virtues or effects.

INCUBUS. A male demon that has sexual intercourse with humans otherwise appears to or oppresses a person. It may also refer to a male demon that materializes in the occult ritual such as a séance.

KABBALAH. The kabbalah is a mystical body of lore, based on an occult interpretation of the Old Testament and other Hebrew religious literature. The term means "acceptance" or "tradition." It is essentially dualistic, having the concept of two opposing principles of good and evil. The most important kabbalistic writing is the Zohar, which appeared in 1300.

LEVITATION. Levitation refers to the rising of physical bodies into the air, beyond the aid of any physical manipulation or agency. The rising is purported to occur through supernatural means. Levitation is found in séances, is often used to authenticate the presence of spirits, and is often used as a form of fortune-telling. It is also a popular occult-oriented party trick.

MAGIC. Included in magic are black, neutral or natural, and white magic. Magic is the use of means (incantations, charms witchcraft), that are believed to be able to secure the compliance or help of supernatural or spirit power. It is the most comprehensive of all the occult terms. The witch, sorcerer, or wizard employs magic in his particular form of occult practice. Magicians are able to read minds and often display a variety of ESP practices; they are also able to attack others through control of demonic spiritual forces. The following are forms of applied magic: spells, healing, disease, love magic, hate magic, magic persecution, defense magic, death magic, and voodoo. White magic differs from black magic in that white witches usually are not intentionally or consciously using satanic power. Black witches and warlocks, on the other hand, give conscious, fanatical allegiance to the devil. The difference lies in the reality of Satan as both and "angel of light" and the "prince of darkness."

MANIFESTATION. A manifestation is the showing or revealing of a demon. This may be in the form of an apparition, ectoplasm, or in the contortions, distortions, or screaming of a demon-possessed person.

MEDITATION. Christian meditation always involves concentrated or reflecting on the law, person, Word, or work of God. Meditation that emphasizes achieving a passive state of mind (often combined with an exposure of the mind to spiritual forces or power) is spiritualistic and demonic in nature. Meditation is common to many forms of the occult, in contrast to biblical prayer, which is always a conscious, intelligent expression of the believer to God. Visions and demonic revelations occurring during the time of meditation are mental tricks played by demons through the imagination.

MESMERISM. Mesmerism, or animal magnetism, is an older term for hypnotism. It essentially has to do with healing of diseases by the use of charms or charming or other magical rituals. Hypnosis may be used in mesmerism, but not necessarily. Healing a cancerous organ by means of stroking a person's hand is an example of mesmerism.

MIND AWARENESS, DYNAMICS, OR EXPANSION GROUPS. Many groups now exist that promise success, fulfillment, increased productivity, and similar results through programs that have occult elements in them. Usually occult meditation is practice in such groups. New and higher levels of awareness or consciousness like the so-called alpha level are generally sought for through the vehicle of a passive or blank state of mind. Many of these groups are aimed at businessmen and middle class housewives. Demon possession often is the end result for the people involved in such groups.

NECROMANCY. Necromancy is a form of fortune-telling in which spirits of the dead (actually demons disguised as spirits of the dead) are conjured up or invoked, often for the purpose of seeking information from them. It can be an attempt to learn of the future from spirits of the dead.

NUMEROLOGY. Numerology is an occult practice in which numbers are interpreted for the purpose of fortune-telling. Numbers are given some kind of magical or superstitious significance. Significant dates in the life of a person may be used by a numerologist to foretell events and/or to describe character traits.

OCCULT. "Occult" means "to hide or conceal," so the occult is that which is hidden or concealed. It also refers to that which is beyond normal perception or knowledge. The occult deals with matters regarded as involving the action or influence of supernatural agencies or some secret knowledge of them.

OMEN. An omen is an observable event or action believed to show the character or nature of a future event. A black cat crossing one's path might be interpreted as a sign or omen of future bad luck.

ORACLE. An oracle is a revelation or message from something supernatural, usually transmitted through a medium. Such a medium might be referred to as an oracle.

OUIJA BOARD. The ouija is a board with the letters of the alphabet on it, together with a small heart-shaped board on casters at two points and a vertical point at a third one (a psychograph) that is used to receive spiritualistic messages and revelations. The occult significance that lies behind the ouija board is not always understood by those who use the board.

PALMISTRY. See Chiromancy.

PARAPSYCHOLOGY. Parapsychology is a branch of psychology that investigates psychical and paranormal phenomena such as visions, apparitions, telekinesis, psychokinesis, clairvoyance, and other extrasensory phenomena. It studies essentially demonic activity. Two major establishments given to the study of such phenomena are the Foundation for the Research into the Nature of Man (FRNM) at Duke University and the London Society for Psychical Research. Parapsychology is the attempt of man to dismiss the true cause of supernatural phenomena. The recognition of the noncorporeal entities is missing in most cases.

PRECOGNITION. Precognition is essentially foreknowledge of the occurrence of events which cannot be inferred from present knowledge. It is clairvoyance as related to a future event or state.

PSI. PSI refers to parapsychological ability—the presence or occurrence of precognition, telepathy, or other psychical or extrasensory perceptions in a person.

PSYCHOGRAPHY. Psychography is the use of an apparatus, like the heart-shaped board (planchette) used with a ouija board, as an instrument for receiving messages from the spirit world. Automatic writing would come under the general heading of psychography.

PSYCHOKINESIS. Psychokinesis or PK has to do with the psychical moving of material objects, objects that are separated or distinct from any source of physical influence on their movement. Demons are responsible for the movement.

PSYCHOMETRY. Psychometry is a form of fortune-telling in which a person (usually a medium) describes a subject's character, whereabouts, ailment, etc., or makes other statements about the subject while holding an article owned by the subject. It is closely associated with clairvoyance.

REINCARNATION. Reincarnation is the belief that living beings possess immortal spirits or souls which at death live on and are eventually reborn in the form of another living being. It is a popular doctrine among occultists, especially among spiritualists.

ROD AND PENDULUM. A rod—divining rod—is an instrument used in fortune¬-telling or in locating objects in a manner beyond the ordinary. A pendulum—like a pendulum in an upright clock—is used as a fortune-telling instrument by spelling out messages or reacting in an unusual manner so that questions are answered or messages are received.

SABBAT. A sabbat, or sabbath, is an assembly or celebration of witches or other occultists, usually held on astrologically significant days or hours.

SATANISM. Satanism is the worship of or religious allegiance to Satan. Examples of Satanism are found in the Process (an organized group of Satanists), Church of Satan and black magic.

SÉANCE. A séance is a meeting of spiritist or spiritualists gathering for the purpose of communicating with spirits (especially spirits of the dead) and/or demons. Usually one member of the group acts as a medium. Participants in a séance usually form a circle and hold hands while standing or sitting. Each participant is to concentrate on the spirit world or assume a passive state of mind. Spirits manifest their presence in any of a variety of ways: speaking through the medium, table rapping, wall thumpings, table lifting or tilting, or other means.

SOOTHSAYING. Soothsaying is a form of fortune-telling through the interpretation of dreams, visions, omens, and other phenomena, Soothsaying, especially in ancient times, were said to have possessed familiar spirits that revealed the sought-for interpretations.

SORCERY. Sorcery is a form of magic in which attempts are made to control or direct spirits. A sorcerer may be referred to as a magician.

SPIRITISM. Spiritism is the belief that mediumistic phenomena are caused by spirits, usually alleged spirits of the dead. Spiritism is very close to animism, in which any and all objects are thought to be indwelt by spirits. Spiritistic phenomena include the following: levitation, apports, materializations, psychokinesis, telekinesis, astral projection, automatic writing, spiritistic visions and speaking in trances, and other. Spiritists believe in the "other side," a realm of bodiless spirits that can communicate with man. One of the main tenets of spiritism is reincarnation.

SPIRITUALISM. Spiritualism is spiritism in a religious context, involving some of the following elements: prayer, Bible reading, hymn singing, preaching, healing, and exorcism.

STICHOMANCY. Stichomancy is a form of fortune-telling by haphazard or random references to a passage or line in a book, even the Bible. God may use a particular Bible verse on a particular page randomly turned to, but this is not a good habit to cultivate. It is rarely true guidance.

STIGMATA. Stigmata are wounds—wounds that may or may not bleed—that are similar to those on the body of Christ (nail marks on hand and foot and/or side). Such wounds are not accounted for by any physical agency. Stigmata may appear on living persons or on statues. Stigmata is unbiblical and strangely mediumistic.

SUCCUBUS. A succubus is a demon assuming a female form, usually for the purpose of engaging in sexual relations with men or women or for the purpose of oppressing a person. It may also refer to a female demon that materializes in an occult ritual such as a séance.

TAROT. The tarot is a form of cartomancy, or fortune-telling by the use of cards. It consists of two sets of cards. One set, called the major Arcanum, consists of twenty-one cards. A second set, called the minor Arcanum, consists of fifty-six cards. Each card is based on an occult symbol and is given an occult interpretation. The tarot assumes that every action and decision is the result of causal law.

TELEKINESIS. Telekinesis refers to the moving of objects where no physical means are involved. Psychokinesis and telekinesis refer to the same phenomenon, but psychokinesis concerns the moving of objects through psychical (mind) processes alone.

TELEPATHY. Telepathy (sometimes redundantly called "mental telepathy") is communicating with or contacting others who may be great distances away without the use of any physical means. Mind reading may also be involved or associated with telepathy. It is thought by some parapsychologists that telepathy is a heightening of a human sense, thereby making it nonspiritual in nature. Telepathy goes beyond the kind of communication and/ or impressions that sometimes occur between persons who are intimately acquainted with each other. Telepathic persons may use their power (spiritual, occult-type power) to control and direct the actions and thoughts of others who are willingly (sometimes unwillingly) cooperating in the telepathic communication. It is clear that telepathy operates through the agency of the demonic. Telepathic communication never brings sure, clear knowledge and is usually shrouded in a vague, mysterious sense of uncertainty.

TRANCE. A trance is a state of hypnotic awareness. There are four forms that a trance may take: light, medium, deep, and stuporous. Mediums customarily enter into trances in which they allow a familiar or guide spirit to control them. Messages, readings, or revelations are usually forthcoming from a medium in a trancelike state. The trance results from the spirit or demon taking full control of the medium, control which the medium has willingly allowed.

TRANSFERENCE. Transference is the process of and indwelling spirit or demon leaving one body and entering another. Spirits or demons inhabiting a human, when cast out, may be transferred to animals or another human, but transferred only according to the acquiescence or willingness of the one on the receiving end.

WARLOCK. A warlock is one given to black magic or sorcery or who has made a pact with the devil. The term "warlock" and "witch" have essentially the same meaning. A warlock may be a man or a woman, but usually warlocks are men and witches are women. A warlock involved in white magic is called a white warlock; one involved in black magic is called a black warlock.

WITCH. A witch—a term usually used in reference to a woman but sometimes to a man—is one given to black magic or sorcery or is one who has made a pact with the devil. A witch is supposed to be possessed with supernatural, generally evil, power.

WITCHCRAFT. Witchcraft is the act of employing magic or sorcery with a good or evil intent. Its purpose is to control spirit or demonic power. A magician engages in magic, or witchcraft; the terms are synonymous.

WIZARD. A wizard is one devoted to black magic or sorcery or one who is skilled in the occult. The terms "witch," "magician," sorcerer," and "wizard" carry very nearly the same meaning.

YOGA. Yoga, or "union," includes various physical and physical-psychical exercises designed to enable one to gain control over bodily processes, possess occult powers, or achieve union with God. Americanizations of Eastern yoga have often centered in the strictly physical (exercise) aspects of yoga without the mystical or occult emphasis of traditional yoga. However, some yoga is combined with astral projection or meditation. Yoga is extremely sexually oriented. Incubi and succubi are common occurrences und the guise of the cosmic mother or father.

Appendix B
Biblical Passages Related to Demonology

Genesis
    3:1–15
    6:1–4
    41:8
    44:5

Exodus
    7:8–13
    7:20–24
    8:6, 7
    8:18, 19
    9:11
    22:18

Leviticus
    17:7
    19:26, 31
    20:6, 27

Numbers
    22:7
    23:23

Deuteronomy
    18:9–14
    18:20–22
    32:17v

Judges
    8:21, 26

1 Samuel
    615:23
    16:14
    18:10
    28:1–25

1 Kings
    5:4
    18:28
    22:19–38

2 Kings
    9:22
    17:17
    21:1–9
    23:5, 24

1 Chronicles
    21:1

2 Chronicles
    33:1–10

Job
    1:1–2
    2:1

Psalms
    78:49
    91:6
    106:36–38

Isaiah
    3:18, 19
    8:19
    14:12–17
    47:11–15

Jeremiah
    27:9

Ezekiel
    21:21
    28:11–19

Daniel
    1:20
    2:2, 27
    4:6–9
    5:7, 11, 15

Hosea
    4:12

Micah
    5:12

Zechariah
    3:1, 2
    10:2

Malachi
    3:5

2 Timothy
  1:7
  2:26
  4:18
Hebrews
  2:14
James
  2:19
  3:15
  4:7
1 Peter
  5:8
2 Peter
  2:4
  2:19
1 John
  2:13
  2:18
  3:8
  3:12
  4:1–4, 6
  5:18
Jude
  1:6
  1:9
Revelation
  2:9
  2:13
  2:24
  3:9
  9:1–11
  9:20, 21
  12:1–13
  13:1–10
  16:13–16
  18:2

19:20
20:1–3
20:4–6
20:7–10
20:14
21:8

CPSIA information can be obtained
at www.ICGtesting.com
Printed in the USA
BVHW091104060423
661866BV00005B/783